FROM WITCH
TO WICCA

ALSO BY LESLIE ELLEN JONES

Myth & Middle-earth: Exploring the Legends Behind J.R.R. Tolkien's The Hobbit & The Lord of the Rings

Druid Shaman Priest: Metaphors of Celtic Paganism

Happy Is the Bride the Sun Shines On: Wedding Beliefs, Traditions, and Customs

✠

FROM WITCH TO WICCA

Leslie Ellen Jones

Cold Spring Press

COLD SPRING PRESS

P.O. Box 284, Cold Spring Harbor, NY 11724
E-mail: Jopenroad@aol.com

Cover art©Daniel Govar, 2004. Check out his fantastic art at:
www.thereandbackagain.net

Printed in the United States of America

CONTENTS

INTRODUCTION

WHAT IS A WITCH? The answer would seem to be self-evident: everyone knows that witches wear pointy black hats, black dresses, and often black cloaks; they fly on broomsticks; their favorite snack is a nice juicy baby; and they are purveyors of potions, curses, and general badness. They are the archetypal villains of fairy tales. Above all, they practice magic.

But there are also the witches of real life, rather than folklore. These may be women—or men—who live on the fringes of society and are blamed for the failure of crops, the milklessness of cows, and the impotence of men. Somewhat similar to the fairytale witch, but minus the costume. Then there are the accused witches, who may or may not have had any knowledge of magic or witchcraft whatsoever, but who were hauled up before various civil and ecclesiastical courts in the medieval and early modern eras, tortured until they confessed to hallucinogenically outrageous acts of depravity, and then burned at the stake or hanged. Already a crack in the definition of "witch" appears: are they monsters or victims?

From the victimized witch springs another image, that of the beautiful, nubile witch whose charms are purely physical. This is the witch as fantasized by witch-hunters, who believe that their own attraction to the "witch" must be coming from the outside, the result of a spell and intended to incite (sexual) evil, and it is also the witch as fantasized by those who wish to see the European witch hunts solely in the context of cultural and institutional misogyny and the Freudian projection of frightening sexual urges.

The victimized witch also generated the theory that "witchcraft" as defined by the witch-hunters was, in fact, a pre-Christian religion practiced in secret for millennia, a theory most strongly associated with folklorist Margaret Murray. Thus, the persecution of witches was not the result of misogyny so much as it was a real crusade against a religion opposed to Christianity. Witches, in this definition, were persecuted as heretics rather than magicians; the Church maligned their deity by labeling him "the Devil." The historian Carlo Ginzburg has pointed out how the blame for inexplicable community misfortunes, such as plagues, shifted from Jews and lepers to witches in the twelfth century, and in many ways Jews and witches have been interchangeable as blameable outsiders. This identification has been adopted in some ways by modern pagans who claim that nine million witches were burned in the witch hunts, a subtle one-upsmanship of the death toll in the Nazi Holocaust hinging on the concept of a burned sacrifice of a class of victims—Jews, witches—to assuage the psychological fears of the mainstream population.

The definition of "witch" becomes even more complex with the emergence of the Wiccan religion, which in most (but not all) of its forms defines itself partly through the practice of magic. Although the public practice of Wicca is less than a century old, there has been controversy among anthropologists and within the religion itself as to how old it really is and what it derives from. The earlier Wiccans claimed, unequivocally, that they practiced the pagan religion identified by Murray. As Murray's theory became discredited within the academic community, however, many Wiccans modified their stance, and most now regard their religion as a new synthesis of authentic ancient beliefs and rituals with contemporary beliefs and concerns, inspired in many ways by Murray's vision of a religion in opposition to the oppressions of mainstream Christianity. In some cases, this has resulted in a religion that gives equal weight to the male and female aspects of the divine, while in others the focus on female divinity is greater. However, Wiccans believe that the practice of magic is a form of worship of the powers of nature rather than a commercial transaction undertaken to manipulate other people; even modern pagans who do not define themselves as Wiccan generally agree with this noncoercive approach to magic.

Central to the definition of the witch is the idea of magic. At some times in human history, the existence of magic has been taken for granted, and at other times it has been ridiculed. Sometimes it is conceived as a purely mechanical, if secret procedure, as formulaic and reliable as a recipe or a chemical experiment. Sometimes it is thought to be an innate spiritual power passed on through a bloodline or an inborn talent like ability in music or mathematics. Some magic heals warts, other magic threatens empires. At any given time, people's definition of the witch is intertwined with what they be-lieve—or wish—magic is capable of accomplishing.

This book is not a history of witches or of witchcraft; there are plenty of those already. Instead, it is a history of what people think witches are. Whether that view has any basis in reality is of secondary concern here. We will begin with the variety of beliefs about witches held by people living primarily in Europe and post-Columbian North America—no offense to the rest of the world, but truly comprehen-sive coverage throughout time and space would take an encyclope-dia—and then look at the ways in which this traditional material has been used, reused, modified, elaborated, and ignored in favor of new creations through the twentieth century and into the present by modern pagans of all stripes, Christian fundamentalists, Hollywood film and television writers and directors, and fantasy writers. The age of science has not eliminated the belief in magic; it has simply reframed the discussion.

One thing that should be understood is that I am not a witch, Wiccan, or Pagan of any stripe. Nor am I a Christian, or a particularly observant Jew. While there is much in modern Paganism that coin-cides with my own beliefs about how the universe works, when it comes to religion, I'm just not a joiner. This book is an outsider's view, based largely on textual sources, and filtered through my background as a mythologist and folklorist.

Thanks are due to Robin Dudley-Howes, Annie RedCrow, and the women of Alegria de la Tierra for allowing me to participate in their 2003 autumn equinox ritual, and to the denizens of All Things Philosophical on *Buffy the Vampire Slayer* and *Angel, the Series* (www.atpobtvs.com), especially shadowkat and Wisewoman, for ongoing discussion about Willow, magic, and witchcraft in the Buffyverse and elsewhere. I have also benefitted greatly from the articles and discussions of modern witchcraft on the Witchvox web site (www.witchvox.com), especially Peg Aloi's insightful and good-natured analyses of witches in film and television.

CHAPTER 1

IN THE BEGINNING, THERE WAS MAGIC

IN THE TWENTY-FIRST CENTURY, "witchcraft" sits uneasily on the boundary between magic and religion. To many practitioners, it is a religion without question, and the rituals they perform are no more or no less magical than the Catholic Mass and just as nurturing of the human spirit. Other modern witches regard what they do more in the light of scientific experimentation—specific actions undertaken to cause specific results, utilizing and channeling natural forces by means of human will. To some people outside of the pagan community, "witch" is a label for a person who worships Satan, sacrifices babies, and is an active force of evil, possibly not even really human. To others, "witch" means a silly adolescent who slept through all the classes where they were supposed to learn how to reason logically and that magic is a fantasy (kids these days; education has certainly gone downhill since I was in high school—I blame it all on television and rock and roll myself).

No one knows when magic or religion began, but both were firmly in existence by the time that humans invented writing because magic pervades early narrative writing. In fact, writing was considered to be a magical skill taught to humans by the gods. Prior to written documentation, however, representation of acts and beliefs in pictoral form—the cave paintings of Lascaux and Altamira, for instance—or in archaeological remains—flowers and ochre in conjunction with a Neanderthal corpse; objects that seem to have no practical use and therefore must have had a "ritual" purpose—are dependent on modern interpretation. Interpretations are made by analogy with beliefs and practices that are documented later or currently found in the same or another culture.

When it comes to very basic, practical activities in ancient preliterate cultures, it is usually fairly easy to interpret the remains—cook pots generally show signs of food on the inside and heat applied to the outside. Religion and magic are much more difficult. An object may be sacred in one context and secular in another: Is this the Holy Grail or a cheap wine glass? An altar or a table? Or both? Or are these people who would use the Holy Grail as ordinary tableware because they don't see any difference between sacred and secular? Or because they regard every meal as sacred? In matters of ancient spiritual beliefs, it is important always to remember that even the most self-evident theories are only provisional and some things really may never be known, short of inventing a time machine.

Modern Western thought sees a real, if fuzzy boundary between magic and religion. A common way of distinguishing the two is to say that a person practicing religion is asking supernatural forces to behave in a certain way and a person practicing magic is trying to make them behave in a certain way. This may describe the difference between a prayer and a spell—a prayer asks for help, while a spell has a specific, predictable result; in either case, if nothing happens, you either did not ask correctly (you were not in the proper spiritual state, or you were asking for something you did not deserve) or you did not act correctly (it was the wrong phase of the moon, or you were trying to effect something that you should not be). However, this is a distinction that exists primarily in the minds of modern academics. Research into the cultures of ancient Mesopotamia and Egypt, for instance, shows that these people considered both "prayer" and "spell" to be "religious" acts. The distinction between magic and religion is artificial in these contexts and in fact can be misleading. Similarly, Europeans who encountered Siberian shamans in the sixteenth century regarded them as magicians, whereas in the twenty-first century shamans are regarded as religious figures. It might be more accurate to say that the distinction between magic and religion at any place or time is that "you practice magic; I practice religion."

Shamanism is probably the earliest surviving form of religion. The classic anthropological study is Mircea Eliade's *Shamanism: Archaic Techniques of Ecstasy* (1964), but Europeans first started to become aware of shamans in the sixteenth and seventeenth centuries, during the era of European exploration—and imperialism—as they encountered tribal peoples in the New World and also in Central Asia. The earliest written references to shamanism, therefore, are the notes and memoirs of early explorers, later of missionaries (by definition hostile witnesses) and merchants. Shamanic peoples themselves were generally preliterate, and so the voices of real shamans were not preserved until shamanic practices were in the process of disappearing under the onslaught of the people who were doing the preserving.

The word "shaman" is the title of religious practitioners among the Tungus tribes of Siberia, but anthropologists have come to apply the word to those who enter into a trance, usually induced through drumming, chanting, and dancing, and send their souls to an Otherworld to interact with spirits and deities. This practice of ecstatic soul-flight is the basic defining element of shamanism. (Some religious scholars make a distinction between shamanistic religions, in which the soul leaves the body to meet the deity on its own turf, and possession religions, such as Vodou or Santería, in which the deity comes down and possess the worshiper's body.) Shamans are found most often in hunting societies, and one of their chief tasks is to negotiate with the Master or Mistress of Animals for good hunting, sometimes striking a deal for how many animals the hunters will kill and promising how the hunters will recompense the deity and the animals themselves for giving up their lives. The other chief function of shamans is to heal the sick, who are conceived as ailing because they are missing all or a part of their souls, lost or held captive in the Otherworld.

Sometimes the shaman's traveling spirit rescues the lost soul in the same way that a hero rescues the damsel in distress, traveling over dangerous terrain, fighting off hostile spirits and other obstacles that block the way, using strength and cunning, and finally bringing the soul home safe and sound. If this sounds like the plot of a folktale, it's no coincidence—folktales may have developed from the stories shamans told their tribes upon their return from the spirit world. The people of the tribe, after all, had no way of knowing what the shaman was doing while in a trance. All they saw was the shaman lying on the ground, seemingly unconscious. When he returned, he had to tell them what had happened, just as traveling traders told stories about their adventures on the road when they got home.

In other circumstances, shamans retrieved lost souls by singing songs that they had learned from the spirits, which charmed the soul or soul-pieces back to the mortal world or induced the spirits to drop their guard so the soul could escape. Often shamans re-enacted the journey to and from the Otherworld while singing the song, turning the soul retrieval into a physical as well as a verbal performance. Trance, in this kind of shamanism, was a less frequent activity and was undertaken to learn from and interact with deities and spirits during down times between healing. In any case, shamanism incorporated and may even have been the origin of all the major arts: music and dance to induce the trance, storytelling, acting, and drawing in the course of relating the shaman's adventures in the moment or after the fact. Furthermore, song in particular was seen as actually originating in the Otherworld, since that is where shamans learned their healing songs; the Otherworld was the source of knowledge in general.

In terms of that distinction between "magic" and "religion," compelling and requesting, shamanism is hard to pin down. Shamans did both: They both came to deities in the role of petitioner, attempting to persuade the supernatural powers to favor the tribe, and also fought with hostile powers in order to wrest from them lost souls and other benefits.

Shamans do not choose their lot in life; they are called, the original meaning of the word "vocation." Joan Halifax's *Shamanic Voices* (1979) is an anthology of personal experience narratives recorded from shamans in a wide variety of cultures throughout the world. It is an enlightening collection in its depiction of the varieties of shamanic experience, but one thread that runs throughout is the trauma of the shaman's call. Before becoming a shaman, the person—male or female, depending on the culture—becomes moody, withdrawn, and depressed. They may become ill themselves, lose a part of their own soul and have to find their own way to the Otherworld to get it back. They may faint or spontaneously drop into trances. They often become healers by healing themselves; having found their way to the Otherworld and become acquainted with its inhabitants, they are now capable of finding their way back.

The shaman's initiation, which takes place in the Otherworld, is literally gut-wrenching: Eliade considered the five important elements of shamanic initiation to be a physical ordeal in which the initiate's body is tortured and torn apart; reduced to a skeleton; viscera and blood replaced; the initiate undergoes a period of teaching in an underworld environment; and finally the initiate ascends to the heavens before returning to the mortal realm. Shamans speak of being dismembered, decapitated, their bones boiled, their own eyes replaced with magic eyes, objects such as crystals inserted into their bodies. They are taken apart and put back together again, slightly different this time. Along the way, they may acquire a spirit lover and/or an animal guide who assists them. They may be taught by spirits and dead shamans in the Otherworld, but they also continue to learn in the mortal world once they have returned, often apprenticing with another shaman.

There has always been a suspicion in European minds that the role of shaman is simply the tribal way of dealing with people whom Western civilization would call schizophrenic, or possibly epileptic, or possibly homosexual (in some cultures, especially American Indian, male shamans dress and act as women, including taking husbands), or possibly whatever else is the mental illness of the month. Certainly the spiritual healing that shamans perform seems to address the kinds of mental issues and the psychosomatic level of illness that Western psychiatry deals with, but if shamans have experienced "mental illness," if the shaman's call is actually a psychotic episode, shamans also heal themselves in the process of accepting their vocation.

Shamanizing is not a question of learning information but of experiencing alternate realities.

Despite their cultural importance, shamans always remain on the periphery of human society, with one foot in the mortal realm and one in the Otherworld. Their power is not always assumed to be benevolent; the one who heals may also be suspected of causing the illness, and failure to heal may have drastic, sometimes fatal consequences. When neighboring tribes are at odds, physical warfare by warriors may be supplemented by spiritual warfare between opposing shamans, and what the shaman does to defend his own people will be viewed as hostile by his opponents. If one group is doing better than another—more successful in hunting, for instance—their shaman may be suspected not only of driving a better bargain with the Master of Animals but also of deliberately thwarting the luck of others. To be a shaman may bring power, but it also brings vulnerability, and it almost always arouses suspicion.

Pure shamanism is today practiced only in cultures that still are or have only recently stopped being tribal. Other religions can only be called at best shamanistic. However, since shamanism is a way of relating to the Otherworld rather than a creed or dogma, elements of shamanism have lingered within cultures, often in areas that have ceased to be identified as religious—that is, in the arts. The possible shamanic origin of the quest tale has already been mentioned. Many Indo-European mythologies also seem to show traces of shamanic experience even when the religion is no longer shamanic. Celtic mythology, in particular, has many elements that seem to speak to a memory of shamanism, especially the violent dismemberment that often befalls poets and bards and the prevalence of journeys to the Otherworld. The story in Germanic myth of Odin's acquisition of the mead of poetry through hanging on a tree for nine days and nine nights, "sacrificing myself to myself," has been seen as a reference to a shamanic initiatory ordeal. Stories in which a character journeys to an Otherworld and returns with valuable knowledge, and stories in which characters undergo physical tests, torments, or loss of limb and yet recover, reassemble, and acquire unusual or supernatural powers may have shamanic origins.

The similarity between shamanic narratives on one hand and myth and folktale on the other, the latter already viewed in derogatory terms in modern Western society, makes it very easy to slip into the assumption that these things are not real. At best, they are "all in the head"; at worst, lies and manipulation for power or profit. It is worth taking a moment to stop and consider the whole notion of Otherworlds and indeed of fiction in the human mind. If, as so much of science insists, the supernatural does not exist and is a figment of our imagination, why does every culture in the world have it? Why does every culture have beliefs in beings that are not animal or human, whether they are called gods, fairies, loa, windigo, or space aliens? Why do all people tell stories about things that have not happened? How do we actually have the capacity to imagine things we have never seen, never *could* see, things that are impossible?

Psychology, psychiatry, neurology, and many other sciences investigate the physical workings of the brain and may indeed someday come to a solution of the "mind-body problem." Many propose characteristics that distinguish humans from other animals—speech, self-reflection, humor, lies. All of these involve taking a step away from immediate reality and, perforce, creating another reality that does not physically, literally exist but occupies a mental— a virtual—space. The things, thoughts, feelings that occupy this space can be profoundly moving and creative (what is creativity but imagining another reality and causing it to come into being?), but can also be frightening, threatening, hostile. It is the space where the things we do not want in our conscious reality reside.

Perhaps the strongest experience most people have of alternate realities is in their dreams. In dreams we encounter beings who are familiar yet alien, people we know to be dead; we fly, fall interminably, walk under water; locations shift and jump; time speeds up and slows down; the images we see have a strange disconnect from the emotions we feel. We think of something and it happens; if we have the ability to dream lucidly, we can control dream events regularly and reliably. It is a reasonable step to wonder whether, since these things happen in dream reality, perhaps they can be accomplished in waking reality as well.

Both religion and magic are extreme exercises in attempting to bring about alternate realities. They proceed from an assumption counter to modern Western thought: instead of labeling only one reality valid, religion and magic (and storytelling and acting and creating visual arts) give equal validity to multiple realities. Even more, the practice of religion and magic attempts to cause one reality to have effect in another. Humans want to bring benefits into their reality from the supernatural realm, but there are ills and evils there as well. People may want to avoid having those things enter their own reality, but there are those who might want to afflict them on their enemies. This gets to the root of the dichotomy of "I practice religion; you practice magic:" I bring benefits (for myself) from the Otherworld, while you may bring evils, which are either benefits for you that do not benefit me, or evils that you wish on me because we are enemies.

The relationship between shamanism and witchcraft is complex. Anthropologists have generally located "shamans" in Asia and the Americas and "witches" in Europe and Africa. Shamanism *is* a society's religion, whereas witchcraft is conceived as existing alongside or in opposition to the dominant religion. In traditional societies, witches are evil and the enemies of humans. In a general sense, they are believed to threaten aspects of fertility: They cause hail, which destroys crops; they cause disease; they make men impotent; they steal cows' milk; they threaten babies and children in almost every imaginable way. In contrast, in an overview article on shamanism published in the *Encyclopedia of Religion* (1987), Eliade noted that "[Shamans] are preeminently the antidemonic champions; they combat not only demons and disease, but also the 'black' magicians. In a general way, it can be said that shamanism defends life, health, fertility, and the world of 'light' against death, disease, sterility, disasters, and the world of 'darkness.'"

Yet there are many aspects of the stereotypical accusations during the witch hunts that bear a strong resemblance to the activities that shamans undertake. Flying, dancing, consorting with the Devil or spirits, having animal familiars or guides, all are typical of both witches and shamans. Carlo Ginzburg's *Ecsatsies: Deciphering the Witches' Sabbath* (1991) outlines many of the analogies between "witches" and "shamans" in Europe, also noting the different moral and cultural weight given to "shamanic" versus "witch" activities. Indeed, the shamans whose beliefs Ginzburg presents held themselves to be fighting against evil witches who threatened the communities' crops. (We will return to these *benandanti* in a later chapter.) However, this witch/shaman opposition can also be seen in the light of the general suspicion of shamanic motives in solely shamanic societies—my shaman is good and defends me, your shaman is evil and threatens me.

The vocation for becoming a shaman comes from within, whether it is sparked by a mental or emotional crisis, a genetic tendency toward trance and other altered states of consciousness that is passed through families, or literally a "calling" from the gods. Shamanism has also been facilitated by the use of drugs such as hallucinogenic mushrooms, ayahuasca, and tobacco, all of which alter the brain's functioning so that the drug taker experiences reality in a different way. One step away from these spontaneous activities is the practice of magic, especially spell-casting, by lay folk.

It seems that in early human society, illness of any kind was regarded as having a supernatural origin. There was the type of illness caused by soul loss, but ailments ranging from the common cold to plague, which modern medicine attributes to germs, viruses, bacteria, and other etiologies, were also cured by the intervention of "magic." These healing magics were as analogous to modern pharmaceutical medicine as shamanism is to modern psychiatry. Periodically, the newspapers are awash with reports that some folk medical remedy does indeed have medicinal value, much to the amazement of all rational people. Garlic, St. Johns wort, kava kava, echinacea, gingko biloba, aloe vera, the whole pharmacopeia of Chinese medicine, and many other substances are tested regularly for their medicinal value. Mainstream medical opinion swings from one extreme to another on the actual value of these folk remedies, but nearly everyone has some remedy or other that they swear by. To some extent, the wonder of modern medicine at the efficacy of traditional medicine is rather condescending—humans could hardly have managed to survive as a species for so long in civilized conditions (so conducive to the spread of germs and viruses) without devising medical cures and procedures that worked to some extent, and most modern pharmaceuticals began, if long ago, as attempts to mimic or improve on the effects of folk medicine.

One sharp distinction between mainstream and folk medicine, however, is that modern American doctors do not tell their patients to recite charms while they take their pills. Insulin works for diabetes because you inject it, no matter what you may be saying while you do, although studies that find a correlation between prayer and recovery from serious illnesses, or mood and the efficacy of a vaccination, may be approaching the realm of folk medical charms. A Slavic cure for fever recorded in 1935 calls for the sufferer to take a piece of baked garlic at dusk, go to the door and look for a fire in the distance, and recite, "There is a fire and there a *vila* [a type of Slavic fairy woman] marries her son and she calls me to the wedding. I cannot go, but I send my fever and a head of garlic." The garlic is thrown in the direction of the light and the patient goes back inside (UCLA Online Archive of Folk Medicine, record 1-1758; www.folkmed.ucla.edu). Any antibiotic effect is completely beside the point in this remedy, as the patient never ingests the garlic. The fever—physical heat—is symbolized by the spicy-hot, baked garlic and a fire belonging to a supernatural being; the charm transfers the patient's heat ("marries" it) to the Otherworld by tossing the garlic head, and this is effected by both word and action. The charm itself is necessary to narrate the desired result; without it, you're simply tossing garlic into the yard.

Early healers no doubt discovered the curative properties of plants and minerals, and these were often used in ways that modern medicine would recognize as therapeutic, but the fact that these items were used to cure transferred a sense of the numinous to the item itself. Without an understanding of why tea made of willow bark eased fever and relieved arthritis (because it contains salicylic acid—the basis of aspirin—which is anti-inflammatory), the willow tree itself was considered to have magical power. Therefore, the willow came to be used in magical formulae in conjunction with charms and spells that are completely divorced from its physical healing properties.

Folk magic works on a few basic principles: Sir James George Frazer, in *The Golden Bough* (1890-1905), called them contagious magic and imitative (homeopathic) magic. They are based on two assumptions: that like attracts like (the Law of Similarity) and that things that have been in physical contact with each other will remain supernaturally connected even after they are physically separated (the Law of Contagion).

Imitative magic creates a desired effect in a person or object by manipulating another object that resembles the focal object in some way. The most classic example of this is the so-called voodoo doll—an object found in European witchcraft centuries before Vodou ever existed. A figure is made that looks like the intended victim and/or contains parts of the victim's body, such as hair or nail clippings; the doll is then mutilated, pierced in specific body parts, burned, or otherwise attacked. The victim is supposed to then suffer the torments that have been inflicted upon the doll.

Contagious magic works by placing two things in contact and then manipulating one of them the way you would like the other to behave. Here the classic example is wart cures. Although there are more wart cures than there are stars in heaven, most of them work by rubbing the wart with something that decays—plant matter, rags—and then placing it somewhere where it will decay—under the house eaves, buried in the ground. As the object decays, so will the wart slowly disappear. All the other wart cures work by rubbing the wart with an object and then abandoning it where someone will pick it up; your warts are then transferred to that person.

While Frazer's anthropological theories have more or less been abandoned, his analysis of the workings of magic is still sound. The garlic-and-fire fever cure uses both contagious and imitative magic: the heat of the objects used (garlic, a distant fire) are imitative, but the fever is cast out when the person suffering makes physical contact by holding the garlic in his or her hand and then throwing it away. The vast network of associations and attributes that are worked on in magical procedures are based on systems of perceived similarities. Fire is hot, fire is red, passion is hot; therefore, passion is red. If you want to manipulate passions—attract love or deflect anger—you use red objects in the spell. If you want to get rid of warts, you touch them with something that will decay as you want the warts to do, but to make it even more effective, use a piece of potato with warty-looking eyes all over it.

Throughout the ancient world, one of the most common forms of magic—or at least the one which has left the best archaeological traces—was cursing. Hoards of curse tablets, called *defixiones*, have been discovered at sites in Sicily, Greece, Rome, North Africa, the Middle East, and Britain, dating from the sixth century B.C.E. through the fourth century C.E. It is most likely that these written curses are merely the latest development of a cursing tradition that began, and probably continued alongside the written form, as an oral performance. Anyone who can speak can perform an oral curse, but only a small percentage of the population could write at this time, so most of the surviving *defixiones* must have been written out for the curser by a professional, though whether a professional witch or merely a professional scribe is open to question.

People cursed for selfish reasons—they cursed their opponents in lawsuits, athletic competition, and business; their rivals in love or straying lovers; or unknown or suspected thieves. Early *defixiones* are relatively simple, consisting of names and little else—presumably the curser spoke the real curse and the *defixione* served as a reminder to the god invoked so they would cause misery for the correct malefactor. Over time, however, curse texts became increasingly elaborate, not only in the detail of the words but they way they are written on the surface—lines alternately going to the left and right, right-side-up and upside-down, embellished with drawings and symbols. The text was written on a piece of lead, a material symbolically associated with the underworld, and the curses were dedicated to a wide range of deities, most of whom lived in or visited the underworld or were otherwise associated with death: Greek Hermes, Persephone, Demeter, Hades, Hecate; Egyptian Thoth and Seth; Jewish Jehovah and Adonai; Babylonian Ereshkigal.

Living in a society that constructs reality through the prism of science, which is above all built on the premise that the universe is ultimately completely knowable (even if we don't know it all quite yet) and visible (even if we can't see it without the aid of equipment, some of which we may not have invented yet), we are taught to overlook the magical and dismiss the working of unseen forces. Science has explained so many things that were previously ascribed to magic that we take it for granted that there is an explanation somewhere for everything. Returning to Frazer, although his evolutionist view of the progression from magic to religion to science, each succeeding stage better and truer than the last, is now regarded as embarrassingly imperialist and racist, his definition of magic as "mistaken science" is so pervasive that we are hardly aware of the bias. Yet if the true nature of reality is something that can only be apprehended through a post-Enlightenment mentality using post-Industrial equipment, then it is surely worthy of note that every society we know of has had a belief in magic and in other worlds, alternate realities.

Once magic is a given, the question remains as to who uses it and to what ends. At the earliest stage in society, it appears that everyone uses it to some extent in order to ensure the successful conduct of daily, personal activities and to effect low-level healing, rather as modern Americans dose themselves with over-the-counter remedies. The most effective practitioners, however, were the shamans, who used it to heal serious illnesses and to benefit the community as a whole. In animistic cultures—those who believe the entire world is alive and filled with spirits, from rocks and dirt to animals and humans to the clouds in the sky and the water in the sea—there are spirits everywhere who might help or hinder your activities, and it is best to be aware of them and to do your best to remain on their good side.

In a world that is hard, harsh, and dangerous, however, an increase in good for one group may cause a decrease in good for another. This concept is called "limited good," the belief that there is a finite quantity of everything and only so much to go around. Even life can be conceived as a limited good: if a person is sick to the point of death, it is sometimes thought that the only way to save that life is to offer another in its place. This is fine for the patient, who gets to live; it is somewhat less so for the sacrificial victim, especially if it was an unwilling victim. The understanding that the benefits of magic are relative seems to have arisen early, as evidenced by spells, charms, prayers, and rituals that do their best to absolve the actors from blame in what happens. Early Greek animal sacrifices, for instance, were designed so that the animal ate food that had already been dedicated to the deity. This was taken either as an indication that the animal freely acquiesced in what was about to happen, or as a "sin" that had to be punished with death. In either case, the sacrificers were no longer to blame for the animal's death.

And so we return to the theorem that "I practice religion, you practice magic." Religion, or at least "my religion" is by definition good for everyone. Magic is ambiguous; it can be good for some but not for others. Religion is altruistic; magic is selfish. Magic can be practiced in benignly selfish ways by everyone, but the more malign the intent, the more likely it is to be practiced by witches.

In some societies, belief in the malignity of witches is so pervasive that they are blamed for every negative event, from eating a less-than-perfect peach to dying a horrid death from a combination of plague, syphilis, and smallpox. (This is actually a rather interesting worldview, since it seems to posit that the natural state of the world would be one of pure bliss, if only there were no witches.) Prior to the advent of monotheism, witches were, by definition, evil beings of malign intent who used magic to their benefit and others' detriment, and religion had nothing to do with it. If witches consort with demons, it is simply because they have common interests.

Indeed, in many African and Asian societies, the Azande among the most famous, witches are hardly human beings at all and seem more like demons themselves: evil beings who are always just out of sight in the shadows and the night until some social tension turns paranoid, reaches critical mass, and erupts in a hysterical mob that lynches a victim who is usually acknowledged, too late, not to have been a witch after all. Newspaper stories show that this type of witch belief still operates in Africa, India, Malaysia, and elsewhere; the news archive of *Fortean Times* magazine (http://www.forteantimes.com) is bursting with such articles. Interestingly, most of the victims are old, solitary, and female.

CHAPTER 2

WITCHES
OF ANTIQUITY

THE NEGATIVE IMAGE OF THE WITCH far predates the European witch hunts of the early modern period, and many of the stereotypes the persist today are seen already in the classical era. For instance, classical witches are invariably female. Males who practice magic may be charlatans, con men, or possibly even genuine holy men, but they are depicted as rational and deliberate, normal if antisocial humans. Witches are irrational, uncontrollable, connected to a force of nature that is outside of society and that threatens it.

There are two types of witch: the alluring, seductive witch who uses her beauty as a trap for the unwary man and then keeps him through magic, and the repulsive, aged witch who uses magic to obtain sex that any man who was not bewitched would never offer her. Sex is always the witch's focus, in one way or another.

Medea is one of the first classical witches, and over the centuries her depiction became ever darker and more threatening. She was one of the beautiful witches, the daughter of King Aeetes of Colchis, an area in what is now the Central Asian country of Georgia. Her father possessed the Golden Fleece, the skin of a supernatural ram which the goddess Nephele sent to save her two children, Phrixus and Helle, from an evil stepmother. The Greek hero Jason had been sent to obtain the fleece for King Pelias, a task that was believed to be impossible (Pelias wanted Jason out of the way). Medea was a priestess of Hecate, the goddess of the crossroads, the underworld, and magic. In the *Argonautica* of Apollonius of Rhodes (mid-third century B.C.E.), Athena, goddess of wisdom, and Hera, goddess of marriage, both of whom had an interest in Jason's success, decided that the best way to ensure that he obtain the fleece would be to enlist the love-goddess Aphrodite and her son, Eros, to make Medea fall in love with the hero.

Having fallen victim to the darts of Eros, Medea used her magic to help Jason perform the impossible tasks set by Aeetes as the condition of taking the fleece: to yoke two bronze-footed, flame-breathing oxen, sow a field with dragon's teeth, and kill the warriors that spring from the ground. Medea prescribed a sacrifice for Jason to perform, which brought him Hecate's favor; gave him a magic ointment to rub over his body, which made him impervious to harm; and gave him the tricky key to distracting the warriors so that he might mow them down. Her skills, therefore, consist of rituals to a goddess, the brewing of magical potions, and insight into the tricks of dealing with supernatural beings.

Up to this point, Medea's actions show supernatural prowess but are (at least from the hero's point of view) beneficial. Aeetes is depicted as being irrationally suspicious and inhospitable within the context of ancient Greek culture. The story seems to apologize for both Medea and Jason: Medea betrays her father because of a spell put upon her by three powerful goddesses (significantly, not the goddess whom she worships); Jason is forced to obtain the fleece by trickery because Aeetes refuses his quite reasonable offer of a trade, the Argonauts' military assistance in exchange for the fleece. However, the question of culpability soon becomes murkier. According to one version of the myth, when Jason and Medea fled Colchis after winning the fleece, Medea brought along her half-brother Absyrtis, and when Aeetes pursued them, killed the boy and chopped him into pieces, which she flung into the ocean behind their ship. Aeetes stopped to recover his son's corpse and thus Medea and Jason made their escape. The two cross the line from animal sacrifice to human sacrifice, a crime that they both must atone for before they may marry and complete the quest.

Apollonius's relatively sympathetic portrayal of Medea ends with the Argonauts' return to Greece. Other works, such as the plays by Euripedes in late fifth century B.C.E. Greece and Seneca the Younger in mid-first century C.E. Rome, concentrate on the aftermath of Medea's arrival in Greece and her marriage to Jason. Here, Medea's use of magic becomes increasingly fatal and vengeful. She tricked the daughters of King Pelias into killing their father by illustrating a youth-restoring spell on Jason's father (from whom Pelias had usurped his throne). This involved slitting his throat and then filling his body back up with a revivifying potion, but when Pelias's daughters slit his throat, Medea did not provide the potion to resurrect him. She and Jason had fourteen children, but Jason eventually left her to make a more politically advantageous marriage to the daughter of Creon of Corinth. Medea turned on her husband, first murdering his new bride with a poisoned robe and crown and then murdering her own children.

Medea spent many years fleeing from one kingdom to another around the Mediterranean, winning over a ruler until her penchant for murder forced to her move on—often in a dragon-drawn chariot. Yet despite her antisocial tendencies, she became an immortal in the Elysian Fields and reigned as Achilles' wife. Many scholars have suggested that Medea herself was a goddess who was debased into a witch in the transition from myth to legend. Whether goddess, priestess, or witch, however, she is a dangerous alien, seductive, powerful, and unpredictable, untrustworthy and at the mercy of her passions. In *Goddesses in Everywoman* (1984), Jungian psychologist Jean Shinoda Bolen presents her as the representation of the dark and destructive side of the Hera archetype, a woman who is so focused on her relationship with a man that, when he abandons her, she takes revenge on everyone except him. From the Greek, male point of view, Medea represents everything dark, dangerous, inexplicable, and frightening in woman. Jason and the Argonauts are more than happy to take advantage of her aid—and she saves their lives on several occasions—yet ultimately, she is always alien, always Other, and always dispensable.

Canidia, the witch satirized by the Roman poet Horace in the late first century B.C.E., is old and repulsive, her magic almost entirely aimed at compelling men to love her. Horace is supposed to have based her on a real woman who was a pharmacist or perfumier, and thus a person likely to have access to the ingredients for potions and poisons. At her first appearance, in *Epode* 5, she and her two equally ugly assistants have kidnapped a young boy, whom they intend to starve to death so that Canidia can use his liver and bone marrow in a potion to regain the affections of her straying lover Varus. She blames Varus's immunity to her previous, less potent spells on the work of some more powerful magic of a rival, and compares her own poisons to those used by Medea to kill her rival in love.

The reader is intended to be repulsed by this scene for a number of reasons. Pity for the boy about to be murdered sets the mood. The women who are planning to kill him are described as looking at him "like a stepmother" (evidently the stereotype of the wicked stepmother was well known in Imperial Rome); Canidia has snakes twined in her hair (like Medusa); Sagana's "rough" hair stands up like boar bristles; Folia's lust is masculine in its strength. These three invert common assumptions about the kind of person who would "naturally" attract love: young, with smooth, shiny hair, delicate, demure. Canidia must use magic to control her lover because no man in his right mind would have sex with her otherwise (and it is clear that it is sex, not love, that she is after).

In the eighth *Satire*, Horace shows Canidia and Sagana digging a pit and ripping open the throat of a lamb to call the spirits of the dead. They use two voodoo dolls, one made of wool and the other of wax, for some unspecified horrid purpose. At the climax of the ritual, however, the statue of the ithyphallic god Priapus in the garden lets loose an enormous fart and the two witches flee in horror, Canidia dropping her false teeth and Sagana her wig in their haste. Finally, in the seventeenth *Epode*, Horace addresses the witch directly, enumerating the symptoms she has inflicted upon him: ashen face, whited hair, endless spasms of pain. He shows all the signs of a man under a malignant spell. He offers any recompense to Canidia for the slanders he has spoken of her, but she will have none of it. His pain will be endless, his death excrutiatingly slow. She recites her magical talents: she can cause death by melting a wax image, draw down the moon from the heavens, evoke the dead, and turn the affections in any way she chooses with her potions.

Horace is probably the first writer to mention the practice of drawing down the moon, a ritual that has become central to modern Wicca. In his worldview, however, it is an unnatural act, removing the celestial object from its proper sphere. Canidia calls on Diana, Proserpina, Hecate, and Tisiphone (one of the Erinyes, or Furies, whose specialty was avenging murder). Her magic, therefore, is achieved through ritual and through calling on goddesses associated with night (Diana as goddess of the moon), the land of the dead (Proserpina) and the underworld in general (Hecate), and one who embodies the kind of blind thirst for vengeance that also motivates Medea.

The image of Medea herself is raised as an example of a powerful, successful witch—one to whom Canidia would like to compare herself. Yet the witches' rituals and spells are undercut by the implicit assumption that an old woman (a vain old woman, or else she wouldn't resort to false hair or teeth) has no right to sexuality and also can have no purpose in life other than the destruction of those who are younger and prettier than she. Her natural fertility gone, she can do nothing but blight the fertility of others, killing youth, consorting with the dead, and inflicting premature old age on Horace himself. Magic, and she who practices it, is represented as deceitful, unnatural, vicious, selfish, and antisocial.

One of the most gruesome witches of all literature is Lucan's Erichtho. She appears in book 6 of his unfinished epic poem *Pharsalia* (written around 60-65 C.E.), which relates the story of the Roman Civil War, approximately one century previously. Lucan lived at the same time as Seneca the Younger (in fact, they died in the same year), and he too had written a (now lost) play about Medea; witches and witchcraft seem to have been a topic of particular interest in the Rome of Nero's reign. Lucan shared Seneca's love of the gruesome, a taste for gore also found in Jacobean drama and low-budget horror flicks. Lucan shows a great disdain for mythology and legend, but at the same time, he is fascinated with the supernatural, the exotic, and, particularly, prophecy.

Before looking closely at Erichtho, it is useful to look at Lucan's description of the Gauls and their Druids. The Gauls are happy when Caesar and the Romans leave because now they can return to their "strange mysteries" and "hateful rites" to "savage," "horrid," and "cruel" gods (book 1, ll. 499-508). A druidic grove is described in book 3, where the trees are covered with blood and their boughs hung with the decaying bodies of sacrificial victims. The chief skill of the Druids, however, is prophecy and divination, and their chief teaching—or at least, the only one of interest to Lucan—is their vision of the happy afterlife. Lucan, however, deems this a false belief, promulgated to deceive warriors into fighting without a healthy fear of death.

Erichtho is given far more space than the Druids, but her description is merely longer and more detailed while retaining the same general tone. She is a witch of Thessaly, a region in Greece renowned for its magic. Here the warrior Sextus, unable to bear the suspense of not knowing his fated outcome in the war, seeks out the witch's divination. Sextus is described as the "unworthy son of a worthy sire" (book 6, l.. 497) whose need for foreknowledge is craven. Not only is his quest cowardly, but he doesn't even do it the right way: he does not consult the oracles at Delos, Delphi, or Dodona, nor does he seek those who read oracles in the flight of birds, in animal sacrifice, or in astrology, sources "lawful though secret" (book 6, l. 512). Instead, he seeks out one "whom no storied witch/ Of fiction e'er transcended" (book 6, ll. 519-520). The inhabitants of Thessaly are so steeped in the black arts that Medea herself came there to fetch poisonous herbs that she could not obtain elsewhere. The gods fulfill the Thessalian witches' requests because their voices are so horrible, it is the only way to shut them up!

The spells that Lucan attributes to these witches as a group are, in general terms, love spells, but of an unnatural kind. They make people love who should not love, their spells overturn even maternal love, and their love-bindings are indissoluble. Underlying this love magic is a serious disruption of the natural order of things: "All things on earth/Change at their bidding; night usurps the day;/The heavens disobey their wonted laws" (book 6, ll. 550-552). From making an old man's heart burn with passion, Lucan's enumeration of the conse-quences of Thessalian witchcraft crescendo into the splitting of the sky, the overturning of gravity, the earth wobbling on its axis. And of all these powerful witches, Erichtho is the fiercest.

Erichtho lives in a tomb so that she has easy access to the bodies of the dead whom she reanimates to gain access to the knowledge housed in the underworld. Her spells blight crops and her breath poisons the air; she raids coffins for body parts and scavenges the hangman's noose, the crucifier's nails from the bodies of criminals. She has no compunction about murdering a human if her spell requires living blood, and she cuts fetuses from pregnant women to offer as burned sacrifices on her altar. She welcomes the war's expansion into Thessaly for the bodies and body parts she will be able to reap from it; indeed, not just any bodies, but noble, well-connected bodies whose souls she can command from the underworld.

Lucan describes Erichtho's search for a suitable body to reanimate in order to answer Sextus's question of when, exactly, he is ordained to die. A new body is better than an old one, because its voice will be stronger and easier to understand. Likewise, it should not have any major injury to the lungs. The reanimation is carried out with the use of potions made of noxious ingredients and the witch's own incantation, a chant that starts out sounding like animal cries—wolves howling, owls screeching, snakes hissing—but slowly evolves into an invocation of deities. She calls upon the Furies first; then Chaos, who mixes worlds into unnatural configurations; Pluto and Proserpine, the rulers of the land of the dead; and Hecate, her patron goddess. She calls the spirit of the dead soldier back to his body, and once he has reluctantly re-entered his flesh, she promises him that if he answers her questions, she will make sure that he will never again be called back to Earth, but will remain peacefully in death. She also assures him that he has not been recalled on a mere whim: "Obscure may be the answers of the gods/By priestess spoken at the holy shrine;/But who braves the oracles of death/In search of truth, should gain a sure response" (book 6, ll. 913-916). After delivering his prophecy, the spirit is still bound to its corpse until Erichtho releases it with magic herbs and chants and burns the body on a funeral pyre.

Erichtho cannot be seen as anything other than a monster (although it is interesting that, after summoning the spirit, she makes sure that it is worth his while in eternal rest). She is physically and morally repugnant, she inverts all normal social life by living amongst corpses, mutilating and desecrating bodies that should be left in peace, working at night rather than by day. She is strongly associated with snakes, which she wears twined in her hair like Canidia, and her patron goddess is Hecate, like Medea. The ritual takes place in a cave, described in gothic terms very similar to Lucan's earlier description of the groves where the Druids carry out their sacrifices. Although she is uniquely loathsome, she is also a compendium of ancient horror's greatest hits. Yet she also anticipates the witches of the early modern era, Shakespeare's weird sisters and the accusations leveled in the witch hunts.

Writing in a non-Christian context, Lucan nonetheless makes a strict distinction between legitimate religion and Erichtho's illegitimate magic. She seeks a prophecy for her client; there are accepted ways of obtaining this information, both through established oracles as at Delphi and through professional (and usually male) diviners who read the future in natural occurrences. Indeed, these diviners may even use animal sacrifice to get their information, so the act of killing in order to obtain knowledge of the future is not itself problematic. However, these courses of action, while legitimate, are also hard to understand and may be misinterpreted. Erichtho's rite gets the information straight from the corpse's mouth, as it were. (Why the dead are presumed to know so much about a future in which they have no part or interest is another question altogether.)

The illegitimacy of Erichtho's witchcraft seems to come from two main sources. First, she uses human bodies rather than animal bodies, thereby tacitly treating "human" as "animal." She thus undercuts the ideological basis of human society, which functions by making an impassable boundary between "nature" and "culture" that corresponds to the boundary between "animal" and "human." Mythologists such as Claude Levi-Strauss believe that the function of mythology is to mediate these categories, cross these boundaries in metaphor if not in fact. Significantly, Lucan dismisses myth as foolish and irrational for precisely this quality of crossing boundaries (like Chaos, whom Erichtho worships).

Second, Erichtho inverts the "natural" order (wherein nurturing women create life by giving birth) through her actions of dismembering dead bodies and creating a being that is, in modern terms, undead (another unnatural crossing of cognitive boundaries). The references to Medea are also significant. True, Medea was an easily recognizable icon of the Bad Witch, but also, within Greek legend, Medea is a woman from Elsewhere, from a more primitive level of culture that the Greeks have outgrown, related to the Greeks but not of them and therefore a potentially dangerous outsider. She represents the irrational and the unknown. For Lucan, Erichtho, the Greek witch, is in the same relationship to his Roman audience that Medea was to a Greek audience. It is ironic that Greece, birthplace of philosophy and logos, here is the location of magic, irrationality, and forbidden knowledge.

Witchcraft gets a somewhat more light-hearted treatment in Lucius Apuleius's *The Golden Ass*, written in the second century C.E. Although Apuleius was writing after the foundation of Christianity and mentions aspects of Christianity in his work, he himself wrote from a purely pagan point of view about a world in which Christianity was a minor cult whose morality and worldview were marginal to society as a whole. Lucius's first-person story tells how he was transformed by witches into an ass for spying on their rites, and after many adventures, how he was returned to his human form through prayer to the goddess Isis, whose votary he became.

The novel begins with the young Lucius traveling through Thessaly, the archetypal home of witches in late antiquity. He came across a man named Aristomenes who told him a story of his own encounter with a witch named Meroë. Aristomenes' story, however, also contains within it the story of Socrates, a man who fell victim to Meroë's spells himself. Socrates had been robbed and was given shelter and then enslaved by Meroë, an innkeeper, who was "no longer young but extraordinarily attractive" (Graves, 1951, p. 7). Socrates described the witch's general powers in melodramatic terms: she can make any man fall in love with her, pull down the sky and thrust up the ground, turn mountains to liquid and rivers to stone, raise the dead and dethrone the gods, extinguish the stars and illuminate the land of the dead. He also enumerated her actual exploits: turning a faithless lover into a beaver and a business rival into a frog, causing ram's horns to sprout from the head of a lawyer who argued a case against her, and cursing the wife of another lover to be perpetually pregnant yet never to give birth. When the townspeople determined to stone her to death, she cast a spell that sealed shut every door and gate in town so that they had to plead with her from the windows to let them free. She only did so when they promised not only to let her live but also to defend her; even so, she retaliated against the instigator of the meeting against her by magically transporting his entire house with him inside it to another town altogether.

Socrates was in the process of running away from Meroë when he met Aristomenes on the road. The two were sharing a room in a tavern in Hypata when Meroë and her assistant, Panthia, magically broke into the room and, before Aristomenes' eyes, slit Socrates' throat, caught all the blood, and then pulled out his heart and replaced it with a sponge enchanted so that it could not pass over running water. The terrified Aristomenes tried to flee the house lest he be blamed for Socrates' murder, but to his surprise, the body jumped up, apparently alive, and Aristomenes dismissed the events of the night as a particularly bad dream. However, the next day, as the two traveled onward, when Socrates tried to drink from a running stream, the slit in his throat re-opened and the sponge fell out, and he dropped dead.

This story sets the stage for Lucius's own adventures in Thessaly. He arrived in Hypata with his head full of stories of magic, inspired both by Aristomenes' story and by Thessaly's reputation as the home of witchcraft and magic. He stayed with a miserly moneylender named Milo, whose wife Pamphilë had a reputation as a witch and a nymphomaniac; the slave-girl Fotis, whom Lucius was soon bedding, described Pamphilë as possessed of "magic arts by which she exacts obedience from ghosts, puts pressure on the stars, blackmails the gods, and keep all the five elements well under her thumb" (Graves, 1951, p. 63). His mother's cousin Byrrhaena, a woman who had nursed him as an infant, warned him that Pamphilë (like Meroë) seduces men for her pleasure and turns violent when rejected, killing the object of her (former) affections or turning him into some kind of animal. Lucius, however, was thrilled to have the opportunity to see some magic for himself. At a dinner party, he heard a story from a man who had been hired to keep watch over a corpse so that witches would not enter the room in the form of weasels, mice, and flies, and gnaw off pieces of its face for use in their spells. While the man, Thelyphron, was keeping watch, a weasel squeezed into the locked and sealed room; when he shooed it away, he was overtaken by a deep sleep. However, he was relieved upon awakening to see that the corpse was unmutilated, despite his failure to keep constant guard.

At the funeral, however, the dead man's uncle charged that the widow had killed his nephew, and to prove it he brought an Egyptian necromancer to reanimate the body and ask it how it had died. When the spell was cast, the corpse reawakened and avowed that, indeed, he had been murdered. Furthermore, when Thelyphron had fallen into that enchanted sleep during his watch, the witches had tried to draw the corpse from the room by calling his name, so that they could get those valuable body parts. Unfortunately, the corpse was also named Thelyphron, and so as they called his name, the watcher Thelyphron had sleepwalked to them, and they had nibbled off his nose and ears and replaced them with wax.

Pamphilë, meanwhile, was casting spells to attract a handsome young Boeotian lover, and sent Fotis to steal some of his hair trimmings when he had gone to the barber. However, because Pamphilë was known as a witch, the barber snatched the stolen locks from her servant, and rather than return empty-handed, Fotis brought back goat hair of the same color, clipped from goatskin wine skins. Then Pamphilë worked her spell:

> When it grew dark, she climbed up to the cock-loft at the top of the house in a great state of excitement, which she finds a convenient place for practicing her art in secret; it's open to all the four winds, with a particularly wide view of the eastern sky. She had everything there ready for her deadly rites: all sorts of aromatic incense, metal plaques engraved with secret signs, beaks and claws of ill-omened birds, various pieces of corpse-flesh—in one place she had arranged the noses and fingers of crucified men, in another the nails that had been driven through their palms and ankles, with bits of flesh still sticking to them—also little bladders of life-blood saved from the men she had murdered and the skulls of criminals who had been thrown to the wild beasts in the ampitheater. She began to repeat certain charms over the still-quivering entrails of some animal or other, dipping them in turn into jars of spring water, cows milk, mountain honey, and mead. Then she plaited the hair

... tied it into peculiar knots, and threw it with a great deal of incense into her charcoal fire (Graves, 1951, p. 65).

Unfortunately, since Fotis had brought hair from wineskins rather than the desired lover, it was the skins that arrived at her door rather than the Boeotian.

Lucius persuaded Fotis to hide him where he could see Pamphilë perform a spell, and he watched her transform herself into an owl by means of a magic ointment. He then persuaded Fotis to bring him the ointment so that he, too, could transform himself into a bird, but the slave-girl mistakenly brought him ointment that turned him into a jackass (and the joke was as good in classical Latin as it is in modern English). Fotis, apologetic, told him that he must eat roses to regain his own form, but from that point on, fate and ill-luck prevented him from doing so until he finally, after many adventures, called upon Isis.

Apuleius's story is consistently played for laughs. He depicts himself as young and foolish, the butt of jokes (he attacks the animated wineskins thinking they are burglars and then falls for an April-Fools-type prank, perpetrated by the entire town, in which he is accused of their murder), and after his transformation, he is the victim of every indignity that can befall a beast of burden. Although Pamphilë and Meroë do not approach the vileness of Erichtho, they are obviously modeled on the same witch stereotype that inspired Lucan. They are witches of Thessaly; they are older women who use magic to sexually entrance younger men; they use body parts stolen from the dead and, even better for their purposes, nails and other objects associated with the execution of criminals; their power is so great that they can command the gods and direct the weather; they can reanimate corpses.

In addition, Apuleius's Thessalian witches are shape-shifters, and it is interesting in light of medieval and early modern European witch beliefs that Pamphilë uses an ointment that allows her to fly, although the ointment does this by transforming her into a bird. Despite Apuleius's satirical tone, however, his witches are to be taken seriously. They are selfish, norm-inverting, inappropriately sexual, vengeful and murderous.

Lucius's jackass state came to an end after he was cast as the lead actor in an obscene religious ritual, wherein he was meant to have sex with a murderess before she was eaten by wild animals. (Lucius is appalled at the prospect of bestiality, but he is even more worried that the wild animals, having eaten the murderess, will go on to eat him as well.) Fleeing the scene of the ritual, he came to the seashore at Cenchreae, and after dipping himself seven times in the ocean, he spontaneously prayed to the Great Goddess to alleviate his misery.

Lucius addressed the goddess by many names—Ceres, Venus, Artemis, Proserpine—"you who wander through many sacred groves and are propitiated with many different rites . . . I beseech you, by whatever name, in whatever aspect, with whatever ceremonies you deign to be invoked" (Graves, 1951, pp. 262-263) to restore his human form, or if his fate is irreversible, to at least grant him death. In response, he had a vision of the goddess herself, who told him that she was "Nature, the universal mother . . . the single manifestation of all gods and goddesses that are" (Graves, 1951, p. 264). She, too, listed many names by which she was known: Pessinuntica among the Phrygians, Cecropian Artemis among the Athenians; Paphian Aphrodite among the Cyprians; Dictynna to the Cretans; Stygian Proserpine to the Sicilians; Mother of the Corn to the Eleusinians; also Juno, Bellona of the Battles, Hecate, Rhamnubia; but her true name was Isis. She told him to attend a procession in her worship on the next day and to eat the rose garland carried by her high priest. As Fotis had told him, it is eating roses that reverses the spell. But since Isis is the one who had finally created the opportunity to do so, Lucius became an initiate in her religion. The last two chapters of Apuleius's novel relate his experience as a priest of Isis and later of Osiris as well, progressing through successive degrees of initiation and becoming, at the deities' behest, a successful lawyer.

The Golden Ass contains many elements of modern Wicca, not in its depiction of witches, but in its depiction of the goddess worship that rescues Lucius from the witches' enchantment. The goddess has many names but is, beneath it all, one goddess, the Queen of Heaven and Mother of All; in fact, she first introduces herself as Nature. Although she has priests, who direct public ceremonies, she appears to her worshipers directly, individually, without mediation. Many of her ceremonies, however serious of purpose, have an element of play and mirth about them. Her worship is initiatory, with degrees and mysteries. Lucius is circumspect about these secrets, but reveals what he is allowed to reveal to the uninitiated: "I approached the very gates of death and set one foot on Proserpine's threshold, yet was permitted to return, rapt through all the elements. At midnight I saw the sun shining as if it were noon; I entered the presence of the gods of the underworld and the gods of the upper-world, stood near and worshiped them" (Graves, 1951, p. 280). This sounds very much like the mystery said to be at the heart of the rites of Eleusis.

Although *The Golden Ass* is presented as a work of light fiction, it is also presented as being, to a certain extent, autobiographical. The hero of the fiction is the author of the novel. The basis of Apuleius's narrative was, in fact, an earlier novel by Lucius of Patra and another by Lucian of Samosata. However, both of those stories used the plot as an excuse for vulgar sexual humor, and although the hero of those tales was equally bent on seeing magic for himself, this seems to be merely a useful plot device to create the hero's humorous plight and occasion some voyeuristic bestiality.

While it is hard to believe that Lucius Apuleius was literally turned into an ass through ill-advised meddling in magic, the author was, in real life, accused of witchcraft and forced to defend himself in court. He had married a wealthy older woman, Aemelia Pudentilla, the widowed mother of an old school friend, Sicinius Pontianus. (She was suffering from some sort of nervous complaint that her doctors told her could only be cured by marriage—like many Victorian doctors, they believed that a lack of sex made women go a little crazy.) Pudentilla soon turned all her wealth over to her new husband, and Pontianus, unfortunately, soon died. Pudentilla's relatives then accused Apuleius of having won her heart by witchcraft and murdered her son to gain all her wealth for himself. Apuleius's defense, which he delivered c. 160 c.e. in the North African city of Sabrata, is known as the *Apologia* or *De magia* (http://www.georgetown.edu/faculty/jod/apuleius/). Although the chronology of Apuleius's writings is uncertain, it is most likely that the accusations and his *Apologia* in response occurred after he had written *The Golden Ass*, and thus his defense of his interest in and practice of magic gives some insight into his life after his initiation into the mysteries of Isis.

First, he was accused of being a handsome philosopher who could speak Greek as well as Latin, used toothpaste, wrote erotic poetry, and owned a mirror. Getting down to the specifics of the accusations of magic, however, Apuleius defined magic as "an art sanctioned by the immortal gods, the instruction in their reverence and worship, a pious art knowing matters divine," and also acknowledged the "vulgar usage" in which a magician is defined as "a man who is able, through a communing with the immortal gods, to cause any miracle he wants with a special power of incantation" (http://www.english.upenn.edu/~schwebel/ap3.html). However, Apuleius also noted that most of the men popularly accused of being magicians, such as Pythagoras, were actually philosophers. His so-called magical rituals were actually scientific experiments; the people who fell down in fits in his presence were epileptics; the secret objects he kept in a napkin on a shrine were religious amulets from his Greek initiations—while he would not reveal them to the public at large, he was willing to show them to anyone else who was an initiate; the poppet he was accused of keeping in secret was a statue of Mercury, publically made and publically worshiped; and the reason his wife, Pudentilla, had not remarried for so long after her first husband's death was not a lack of desire for marriage, but a lack of desire for the man her late husband's relatives tried to force on her, in order to keep her money in the family.

Apuleius thus placed "real" magic in the realm of religious worship and implicitly equated magicians with priests. However, the accusations of selfish, illicit magic made against him were all shown to be foolish (he had shiny teeth! he purchased fish!) or false (not only had he not profited by his marriage, he had encouraged his wife to leave her money to her children, even when they behaved badly over her remarriage).

Several things become clear in contrasting the magical accusations against Apuleius with the depictions of fictional witches in ancient literature. Apuleius was accused of being, like other (male) magicians of the ancient world such as Apollonius of Tyana and Simon Magus, a charlatan who used the cultural belief in magic for his financial benefit—in other words, a rational, cold-eyed con artist.

Witches such as Medea, Erichtho, and Pamphilë, however, used their magic for sexual gratification, and their vengeance was equally passionate. Male magicians practiced sleight-of-hand and prophesied in public and in the light of day; female witches practiced in private, in graveyards, and at night. Really good male magicians convinced their followers that they were gods, sons of gods (Jesus Christ was viewed as a mere magician by some—all those showy miracles), or had a direct line to the gods. Female witches overthrew the gods, made the gods bend to their will. The magic of male magicians was religion gone bad; the magic of female witches was sacrilege. (Remember that Medea's magic was acceptable while she was still a dutiful priestess of Hecate, and she became an uncontrollable horror when she succumbed to sexual infatuation and used her powers for selfish purposes.)

Most importantly, while male magicians were petty criminals, a blight on society, female witches threatened to overturn all nature and society and return the cosmos to primal chaos.

CHAPTER 3

THE DAEMONIC REALMS

By THE BEGINNING OF THE CHRISTIAN ERA, there was already a sharp divide between fictional or mythic witches, who embodied all the fears of masculine Roman society, and the real-life purveyors of folk medicine and love potions. In a society that was not only polytheistic but multicultural, the lines between religion and magic constantly shifted. It was, in fact, an age of miracles, even if most of them were staged. The existence of ecstatic cults with their roots in archaic shamanism, however, kept the possibility of real magic and real contact with Otherworlds always at least theoretically present.

The Late Antique world offered the greatest religious eclecticism the Western world would see until the twentieth century. In addition to the ordered hierarchies of the Greek and Roman pantheons, headed by father gods and functioning like patriarchal families, there were also religions focused on mother goddesses accompanied by sons or younger lovers, such as Cybele and Attis, religions focused on mother-daughter dyads, such as Demeter and Persephone, religions focused on co-equal male and female deities, such as Baal and Astarte, religions focused on single deities, such as Mithras or Yahweh. Few religions required exclusive adherence, and any religion within the Roman Empire had to coexist with the state religion, which maintained the equilibrium of the social cosmos. The uniqueness of Christianity within this religious environment was not so much the teachings of Jesus as the religion's increasing intolerance of other religions. Even rigidly monotheistic Judaism coexisted with the other religions of the Mediterranean world; it simply looked down its nose upon the Unchosen. Not only were Christians prevented from participating in any other religious practices, but by the Middle Ages, Christians wanted to prevent anyone else from participating in any other religious practices, too.

The transition from a world in which magic was good or evil depending on its intent and outcome to one in which magic was by definition evil was slow, and took place largely in the Mediterranean world within the purview of the Roman Empire. In a large part, it evolved from a contrast between the sophisticated religious outlook of the city folk and the quaint customs of the rural peasants, or pagans (people who lived in the *pagus*—the country). The religious eclecticism of Late Antiquity was focused in the cities, where people from all over the known world mixed together. Here, there were numerous different religions that coexisted side by side and interacted with each other, yet still retained their individual integrity.

In the countryside, religious society was more stratified. Throughout most of the empire, a Roman upper class reformulated the local and native religion into Latin form and religious options were more limited. Archaeological evidence from the Celtic realms of Rome— Gaul and Britain—shows that the local Celtic deities were usually given Roman consorts so as to be worshiped as a divine couple, such as the Celtic goddess Rosmerta and Roman Mercury, or the name of the Celtic deity was hyphenated with the name of a Roman deity, such as Apollo Grannus or Sulis Minerva. The locals worshiped these gods in, apparently, more or less the same way they always had before incorporation into the empire; the major change aside from the names was the adoption of permanent temples and statues depicting the gods. Temples to the more exotic deities, such as Mithras, are found only at army outposts or in cosmopolitan centers such as London—places populated by outsiders.

In the cities, the variety of religions meant that multiple interpretations of the nature of deity and of other supernatural concepts were available. One particularly useful concept was the *daimon*, originally a Greek term for an entity or force that occupied a spiritual position halfway between gods and humans—not quite as powerful as a deity, but much more so than a person. Their moral and ethical status was ambiguous. In some cases, they could be messengers from the gods to humans; sometimes the message they carried was good, sometimes it was bad. *Daimons* might act on their own behalf, helpfully toward a human who had taken their fancy, disruptively when they just wanted some fun. Patrick Harpur, in his thought-provoking book *Daimonic Reality: A Field Guide to the Otherworld* (1994), sees *daimons* underlying most of the "weird stuff" that modern science cannot account for—fairies, angels, phantom hitchhikers, abducting aliens.

The Greeks believed that everyone had a *daimon* assigned to them at birth, the actions of which formed the person's individual destiny—a concept adopted by Philip Pullman in his trilogy of children's novels, *His Dark Materials* (1995-2000). Carl Jung had personal experience of his *daimon*, a being who looked like an old man with wings and bull horns, named Philemon. Although Philemon first appeared to Jung in a dream, the psychologist strongly felt that Philemon was a consciousness and a being quite outside of and separate from himself. This was no dream projection, wish fulfillment, or creative visualization. Plotinus, the founder of Neoplatonism, who lived in the third century C.E., was said to have been talked into attending a ritual in which his personal *daimon* would be invoked—it seems to have been the Late Antique version of a seance or a past-life regression session—and, much to everyone's embarrassment, Plotinus's *daimon* turned out to be a god. While *daimons* are intermediate between humans and deities, clearly some are closer to one end of the spectrum than others.

Harpur uses "*daimon*" as a useful shorthand term for all of the lesser spirits and beings that populate folklore and mythology. They are the beings that animate the physical world; the naiads, dryads, and *genii loci* of classical myth; the trolls under bridges and the fairies at the bottom of gardens. They are also what hides your car keys and then redeposits them in a place you looked in five times already. (Immediately after writing this paragraph, my watch disappeared for two days and rematerialized in exactly the place I knew I left it, and where I had looked half a dozen times. I think *daimons* are just swell, really.) They are the brownies who clean the house at night and the goblins who steal children and replace them with sickly, peevish changelings. They are the shaman's spirit guides. They are the tortoise sent by God to tell humans that they would always live, and the hare who got there first with the message that humans would always die. They were also, in Late Antiquity, a very useful concept for describing the supernatural forces of a religion other than your own, forces that you were not prepared to give equal status with your own deity, but who were clearly more than human and more than imaginary.

The *daimon* was an important concept in Neoplatonism, the last great philosophy of the ancient world that persisted until the sixth century C.E.; it was the dominant philosophy during the era in which Christianity became the dominant religion in Europe and, as a result, was highly influential in Christianity's evolving theology. Neoplatonism conceived of the universe as consisting of a hierarchy of levels of being, the lowest of which was the physical world. Each level of being both is derived from the level immediately above it and strives to return to that level, with the ultimate goal of working its way up to the topmost level, the One or the Good. The hierarchy of being can also be conceived as a pyramid, with the unitary Good at its apex and increasing diversity and multiplicity of being as the levels recede toward the physical world. Thus, each level of being is an image of the level above it, and the level above provides the archetypes for the multiple images in the level below. *Daimons* are, then, how we humans perceive the beings of the level(s) above the physical world, and as they belong to higher levels of being, they are correspondingly less physical, but nonetheless just as real, as beings that inhabit our physical realm.

Between the physical world and the Good was the space in which resided the gods and *daimons*, which the Neoplatonists called the *Anima Mundi*, "the world-soul." The *daimon* moved between this level and the material world as a messenger (*angelos* in Greek) between gods and humans. Christianity adopted this idea of *daimonic* mediation, but divided these incorporeal spiritual beings into two classes: angels, who carried messages from God, and demons, who served the Devil. Or, once again, the (good) *daimons* of "my religion" and the (bad) *daimons* of "your superstition."

After the incredible diversity of religions that coexisted during the Roman Empire, the religious pendulum swung to the other extreme as Christianity steamrolled its way through Europe, with the aim of becoming a universal, monolithic religion. Before assessing whether this project was successful, however, it is necessary to consider what reasons Europeans had for converting to Christianity. This is a question that has been often overlooked or taken as given in histories written from a Christian perspective, whether that stance is taken consciously or unconsciously. Until recently, any European or American perspective after the early Middle Ages had to be colored by the fact that Christianity *had* triumphed and, moreover, has such an enormous cultural impact that it is almost impossible to make distinctions between "European" and "Christian" culture, just as it is virtually impossible to make any distinction between "American" and "capitalist" culture.

Christianity arose in urban, Mediterranean society. It is usually claimed that the religion's great appeal was its democracy—anyone could join, and all Christians have equal potential for sanctity, regardless of gender, status, or wealth—and its promise of a heavenly reward no matter what sufferings one endured on Earth. It is often characterized, in its early years, as a religion of the disenfranchised: women and slaves. Its emphasis on gentleness, charity, and love is contrasted with the more savage and bloody alternatives such as the cult of Cybele, or the essentially political, or at least non-mystical state cult that worshiped the Emperor. Its promise of intangible benefits in the world beyond are contrasted with the earthly benefits offered by pagan cults, which in this picture are implicitly or explicitly seen as vulgar, simple-minded, unrefined, and unenlightened.

Richard Fletcher's study of *The Barbarian Conversion from Paganism to Christianity* (1997) shows that these dimensions of Christianity may have had meaning in the urban society of the Mediterranean world, but were less of an incentive for the conversion of northern Europe. As Christianity became the dominant religion of the Roman Empire and its immediate heirs, Christianity became synonymous with a whole host of other, nonreligious qualities: power, political influence, literacy, organization (a not inconsiderable quality in a world devolving into chaos), sophistication, and, in general, high status. Throughout northern Europe, conversion was often a condition for a pagan king making a political alliance with a (more powerful) Christian king. Christian princesses were married off to pagans and the priests who accompanied them to their new courts used their positions to proselytize. The political and material successes of Christian rulers were invariably attributed (by them and by others) to their faith, making Christianity seem like a good bet for getting ahead in the world.

When kings converted, their subjects, willy-nilly, did too. While conversion might have political benefits for the ruling class, Christianity's benefits for the common folk were often less evident. Fletcher references the sociological concept of "empirical religiosity" to describe the religion of the pagan rural folk—religion was supposed to provide tangible benefits in the form of good health, abundant crops, increasing herds, chubby babies, and eternal fame. The benefits of Christianity were much less tangible. The early Church was aware that, while some people experienced the classic conversion experience like Saul on the road to Damascus, a sudden blast of enlightenment that radically changes a person's experience of the world, for others it was a slower process. Therefore, as Pope Gregory advised Augustine on his mission to Britain:

> . . . . the temples of the idols among that people are on no account to be destroyed. The idols are to be destroyed, but the temples themselves are to be aspersed with holy water, altars set up in them, and relics deposited there. . . . In this way, we hope that the people, seeing that their temples are not destroyed, may abandon their error and, flocking more readily to their accustomed resorts, may come to know and adore the true God. And since they have a custom of sacrificing many oxen to demons, let some other solemnity be substituted in its place . . . On such occasions they may well construct shelters of boughs for themselves around the churches that once were temples, and celebrate solemnity with devout feasting (Bede, 1968, pp. 86-87).

The process of Christianization, then, started by telling "the folk" that they had been on the right track with their old religion, but they had been worshiping the wrong gods. The structure of the old religion was to remain; only the deity (and the liturgy) changed. Meanwhile, new generations were raised in Christianity from the beginning. The accommodations that the missionaries made with paganism in order to make the conversions, however, left the folk with ambiguous messages about the relationship between their old practices and the new religion. Conversion, once achieved, was not necessarily retained. Some kings, such as Raedwald of East Anglia in the late sixth or early seventh century, converted to Christianity under the influence of Edwin of Northumbria, and then returned to paganism, or perhaps practiced both Anglo-Saxon paganism and Christianity side by side. Also in the late sixth century, Gregory of Tours encountered a Spaniard who mentioned (to the bishop's outrage) that it was common in Visigothic Spain to worship at both pagan and Christian altars. Archaeological remains, especially decorative artwork, attest to this mixing of pagan and Christian themes.

Furthermore, the fact that in northern Europe Christianity was very much imposed from above—as opposed to the Mediterranean cities, where people had converted by personal choice and the religion spread from below—opened a religious chasm between the upper and lower classes that had not existed before. Furthermore, for people who spoke Celtic, Germanic, and Slavic languages, the experience of Christianity conducted in the elite and alien language of Latin was very different from the experience of lower-class people whose native language was Latin or something very close to it, languages in the early stages of diverging from Latin into Romance vernaculars. Although missionaries preached and converted in the northern European vernaculars, throughout the Middle Ages there was a self-evident contrast between "sacred speech" and "secular speech" beginning with the language in which each was spoken.

Fletcher notes that the early medieval missionaries who set out to evangelize the countryside faced formidable challenges:

> Historians have often written dismissively of "pagan survivals," old beliefs and practices tolerated by a sagely easy-going church, which would

subside harmlessly into the quaint and folkloric. But this is to miss the point. The men of the sixth century—and not just the sixth century by any means—were engaged in an urgent and competitive enterprise. In a European countryside where over hundreds of years diverse rituals had evolved for coping with the forces of nature, Christian holy men had to show that they had access to more efficacious power. . . . Country people are notoriously conservative. We may be absolutely certain that more than a few generations of episcopal exhortation or lordly harassment would be needed to alter habits inherited from time immemorial. Ways of doing things, ways that grindingly poor people living at subsistence level had devised for managing their visible and invisible environments, were not going to yield easily, perhaps were not going to yield at all, to ecclesiastical injunction (Fletcher, 1997, p. 64).

The Christianization process was slow, and throughout most of the Middle Ages it could be argued that the religion practiced by laypeople was far closer to their former pagan practices than that practiced by the Church elite and the upper classes from which that elite was drawn. At the same time, what the folk practiced was not merely paganism with a thin Christian veneer. The medieval European peasantry reinterpreted their religion within a Christian framework, substituted a new set of powerful beings (God, Jesus, Mary, and the saints) for the old ones (the pagan pantheons), and, as always, did their best to remain healthy, wealthy, and wise.

The discrepancies between elite and popular theology, however, set the stage for conflicts. Once again, churchmen inspired with reforming zeal found themselves bound to eradicate "your superstition" in favor of "my religion." A case in point is the matter of St. Guinefort, the holy greyhound. Stephen de Bourbon was a noted preacher and inquisitor in the districts of Lyonnais, Burgundy, Franche-Comté, Savoy, Champagne, Lorraine, Auvergne, Languedoc, and Roussillon; he also wrote extensively on the various heretical cults and superstitions he encountered in his work as an inquisitor. In the region of Lyon, he encountered a healing cult focused on this saint, which was a loyal dog who saved the master's baby from a snake, only to be killed under the mistaken belief that he had attacked the child himself. (This is, in fact, a popular folktale motif; a nearly identical story is told to explain the placename Beddgelert (Gelert's grave) in North Wales. The dog Gelert was slain by his master Llewyelyn ap Iorwerth, one of the great heroes of medieval Wales, who lived, perhaps significantly, approximately a generation before Stephen de Bourbon encountered the Guinefort cult in France—the story was apparently going the rounds in early thirteenth century Europe.) The martyred dog was adopted as protective patron, and women brought their ailing children to his shrine to be healed. Stephen briskly relates how he put a stop to that nonsense, thank you very much, digging up the dog's bones and burning them along with the grove of trees which surrounded the shrine.

Women especially, with sick or poor children, carried them to the place, and went off a league to another nearby castle where an old woman could teach them a ritual for making offerings and invocations to the demons and lead them to the right spot. When they got there, they offered salt and certain other things, hung the child's little clothes (diapers?) on the bramble bushes around, fixing them on the thorns. They then put the naked baby through the opening between the trunks of two trees, the mother standing on one side and throwing her child nine times to the old woman on the other side, while invoking the demons to adjure the fauns in the wood of "Rimite" to take the sick and failing child which they said belonged to them (the fauns) and return to them their own child big, plump, live and healthy. Once this was done, the killer mothers took the baby and placed it naked at the foot of the tree on the straws of a cradle, lit at both ends two candles a thumbsbreadth thick with fire they had brought with them and fastened them on the trunk above. Then, while the candles were consumed, they went far enough away that they could neither hear nor see the child. In this way the burning candles burned up and killed a number of babies, as we have heard from others in the same place. (*Internet Medieval Sourcebook,* http://www.fordham.edu/halsall/source/guinefort.html).

This ritual, passing a sick child between two trees or through a split tree trunk and chanting an invocation to some supernatural power, is found in European and American folklore into the early twentieth century. It was used to cure colds, wasting sicknesses, infertility, whooping cough, hernias, rheumatism, tuberculosis, and many other ailments. The idea that an ailing child must be a changeling left by the fairies (or "fauns," as Stephen calls them) who must be entreated to return the real, healthy baby, is also widespread, as is the use of fire or the threat of fire to force the fairies to make the switch. To Stephen, however, "They were seduced and often cheated by the Devil so that he might in this way lead men into error" (ibid.).

The reforming outsider saw these practices as superstitions and evidence of the Devil's wiles, but presumably there were other priests working in the area who were not so disturbed by these practices as to do anything about them, even if they may not have approved. It is worth noting, however, that this cult was concerned with healing, an extremely gray area in the distinction between the religious and secular realms. This particular ritual works purely in the realm of magic, creating circumstances in which supernatural intervention is possible, indeed inevitable. It would take only a very slight change, however, to move into the realm of folk medicine, by the application of some healing herb or potion that might actually have medicinal properties in addition to the ritual, whereby the ritual sets up the circumstances for the medicine to work, assisted by supernatural powers.

The transition from paganism to Christianity in Northern Europe has generally been viewed through one of two lenses. In the first, the slate is wiped clean, erasing paganism (or perhaps turning it into a chalky blur with only a few faint outlines still visible) and rewriting the religious lesson from scratch in Christian terms. Implicit in this view is a sudden change of mindset in which the old worldview is completely and utterly rejected. In the second, Christianity is a thin veneer applied over an eternal paganism, which may still be glimpsed through cracks and chips in the surface. The milder form of this view regards the peasantry as too simpleminded to bother changing their beliefs, just going along with orders from the manor, while the more extreme form sees the Christian veneer as part of an active conspiracy to hide a deliberate paganism.

This latter might be termed the Margaret Murray view, as expounded in her books *The Witch Cult In Western Europe* (1921), *The God of the Witches* (1933), and *The Divine King in England* (1954). The problem with Murray's thesis in its most extreme form—that up to the sixteenth century, essentially all of northwestern Europe was actively pagan, from the top of society down to its roots, and just pretending to be Christian for appearances' sake—is that, if it were true, why would anyone need to hide their paganism? The most the Pope could do was excommunicate everyone, and if they weren't actually Christian to begin with, why would that bother them? The opinions of Christians about your theological purity only matter if you are a Christian already.

The actual state of affairs, as scholars have increasingly realized over the last twenty years, is that, pagan or Christian, human beings have the same basic needs and interests. What is important is that the crops grow—as a pagan, you might pray to Nerthus, and as a Christian, you might ask a saint to intervene, but the need and the intention remain the same. The problematic area, as Fletcher notes, is convincing people that Jesus is as effective as Odin, because when the stakes are high, people tend to believe that if it ain't broke, don't fix it. They also tend to believe that if one is good, two is better, so like Raedwald of East Anglia, they will hedge their bets by praying to both Jesus and Odin, just in case. For a very few people, the fine points of theology are important; for most, religion is a practical matter and results are what count.

Furthermore, outside of movies, people don't get knocked on the head and suddenly undergo a complete change of personality, an utter loss of memory, and still manage to function in the world. Even the most Pauline of conversions leaves the convert with a mental structure, a way of approaching the world, conditioned by former beliefs. They may respond to conversion by actively and consciously rejecting, inverting, and denouncing their former beliefs, but those beliefs are still active, although in a negative rather than a positive way. Many of the features of early Christianity, for instance, were designed specifically to differentiate Christianity from Judaism—no, we have our Sabbath on Sunday, not Saturday—even as they served to blur the distinctions between Christianity and other religions of the Roman Empire (what do you know, our god was born on December 25, too!). Interestingly, the Roman religions that Christianity most came to resemble, such as the cults of Sol Invictus and of Mithras, were highly masculine religions which, in some cases, did not even allow women to join, while the religions it most came to reject were the female, goddess-centered cults.

The conversion of northwestern Europe was not, it seems, a case of the population suddenly seeing the error of their ways and ceasing to want one set of (pagan) benefits in favor of another set of (Christian) virtues, but rather of people wanting the same things from their religions and trying to get them in the same way, but seeking them from a different set of supernatural beings. It was completely possible to be a Christian and still believe that you cured sickly babies by passing them through holes in rocks, or cured lameness by tossing a leg-shaped votive token into a holy well. It was also possible to be a Christian and believe that your bad luck was due to the malevolence of your neighbors, who were calling on powerful supernatural beings to assist them in taking what was rightfully yours, or summoning hailstorms to destroy your crops, or making your cows go dry. God, after all, was very far away; Jesus was somewhat nearer, and the saints were closest of all, but the closer they were, the more limited their power.

An Anglo-Saxon mnemonic poem called "The Lay of the Nine Twigs of Woden," which was apparently used to remember remedies for poisons, refers to both the Germanic god Woden/Odin and to Christ, as well as to "the wise Lord/Holy in heaven when He hung," which could be either Christ or Odin. A blessing of the fields, or *æcerbot*, requires masses to be said and Latin prayers recited over sods from the field, and also appears to invoke the earth goddess to be fruitful. Karen Jolly, in whose *Popular Religion in Late Saxon England: Elf Charms in Context* (1996) these charms appear, notes that the appearance of "pagan" elements in "Christian" curing charms indicates not that Christianity failed in its attempt to overwrite paganism, but that it succeeded in the task, set by Pope Gregory, of assimilating it:

> [T]he similarity in worldview between late Antique Christianity and pre-Christian Anglo-Saxon culture enhanced this acculturation process. Germanic animism, with its sacred trees, wells, and stones, and early Christianity, with its Neoplatonic world and cult of dead saints, shared a common outlook on the intimate connection between the spiritual and the material. . . . Between, then, the extremes of magic and miracle that

> exemplify the conflict between pagan and Christian beliefs, stand these middle practices, remedies that meet the practical, everyday needs of a rural population with a new synthetic tradition mediated by the growing body of local clergy. (Jolly, p. 171)

Pagan priests were eliminated but the daily magic continued. Bereft of any ritual context, myths and hymns turned into legends and poetry, often preserved by monastic scribes. Where formerly an organized clerical body, such as the Druids, oversaw all aspects of cultural knowledge, under Christianity, cultural tasks became specialized. The Church was in charge of religion, while the State evolved to take charge of law (although ecclesiastical and secular law coexisted for many centuries and often came into jurisdictional conflict). The historical epics that legitimated the culture were still recited, but by poets who were no longer priests. Healers, too, were no longer necessarily sacred—although this was another area where conflict between ecclesiastical and secular authority might clash. "Natural philosophy" or the understanding and investigation of the natural world remained in the realm of religion, but was now refracted through the lens of the Bible rather than that of pagan cosmology.

An Irish legend about the origin of the role of the scribe shows how pagan, Druidic knowledge was dismantled by Christianity, which kept some bits of paganism that seemed to be useful and discarded others. (As a result, the cultural glue that held Druidism together as a whole was lost, leaving only enigmatic fragments behind.). The twelfth century *Auraicept na n-Éces*, the "primer for poets," contains an Irish grammar, a collection of poetic meters, and illustrations of a myriad of ogham alphabets—a form of runic alphabet formed with notches cut on the edge of a four-sided stick. The contents of the *Auraicept* lead to the suspicion that the monks had a little too much time on their hands one day in the scriptorium—sow ogham, in which each letter is the name of a different kind of pig? Bird ogham, dog ogham, king ogham, river-pool ogham? Oghams that turn around in spirals?

The *Auraicept* was supposed to have been written by one Cennfaeladh, son of Aillil, who suffered a head wound in the Battle of Magh Rath c. 634, so that he lost his "brain of forgetfulness." After he was cured, he lived at the meeting of three roads; down one was a school of Brehon law, down another a school of poetry, and down the third a school of Christian learning. Cennfaeladh studied with each in turn, and every night he wrote down everything he remembered in a book.

Now, Celtic learning was traditionally oral—the Druids forbade writing to be used for anything other than keeping business accounts—so Cennfaeladh's note-taking was an important break with the past. The implication of the story seems to be that, because of his head injury, he could not forget anything, although it is more likely that someone who lost a large chunk of his "back brain" would have trouble remembering, and therefore would need to write things down because he was unable to memorize. As it stands, however, the story presents the image of a brain that has become so crammed tight with data that the only way Cennfaeladh could function was to "download" it into a book.

More importantly, Cennfaeladh has to go to three separate schools. One teaches law, which had formerly been the province of the Druids, and this school is separate from the school of Christian learning, which makes the secular nature of the law all the more evident—this is not canon law Cennfaeladh is learning. Another is a school of poetry, also the province of Druids and also a skill strongly related to magic. The final school is decidedly *not* druidic but Christian, and we can assume that it has replaced the purely pagan element of Irish learning. Nonetheless, although one-third of the Druids' wisdom has been ousted by Christianity, two-thirds remain. In a like manner, the Brehon law itself was supposedly revised by Saint Patrick, who took out all the laws that were contrary to Christian morals but left in whatever was "wholesome."

Paganism persisted, then, fragmented and heavily edited, leaking out of a man with a hole in his head. Brain damaged as he was, however, he couldn't forget the past, and he also couldn't forget the present.

The process of selectively replacing pagan beliefs and practices with Christian ones was especially urgent in the realm of "magic." First of all, becoming Christian implicitly meant redefining as both magical and dangerous many practices, such as healing, which were not necessarily religious in a theological sense but which were carried out with reference to supernatural powers. Even within the clergy there was a wide spectrum of opinion as to how much accommodation with pagan beliefs and practices was acceptable. As a general rule, however, it was the clergy at the highest and most intellectual levels who were outraged at any hint of accommodation, while it was the priests who actually lived among the people who saw the persistence of ancient festivals and cures as harmless, as long as people showed up in church as well.

As Valerie Flint shows in *The Rise of Magic in Early Medieval Europe* (1991), the overall trend was for Christianity to accept "the magic of the heavens" as assimilable to a Christian worldview, while "the magic of the earth" was dangerous and unacceptable. In part, this appears to be a very elitist stance. Neoplatonism and its philosophy of the spheres was intellectual and Roman; it provided the opportunity for as much theological finesse as the question of the nature of the Trinity. It was heady stuff, incorporeal and non-smelly. Earth magic, however, was physical, messy, and usually involved women. It was aimed at increasing factors that good Christians should be trying to turn their minds from, not toward: wealth, health, luxury, love. It was practical and aimed at doing, whereas heavenly magic was abstract and aimed at understanding.

What this really broke down to was that Christianity accepted *daimons* and rejected demons. The whole concept of *daimon* and demon was extremely useful, however. Where the pagan philosophers had seen *daimon* as a single category containing both good and bad (or helpful and harmful) entities, Christians tweaked the concept and created two categories: good entities—angels—and bad ones—demons. Likewise, the study of astrology was rehabilitated. First of all, it was concerned with the realm of the heavens, and therefore of the region closest to God, and second, it consisted of the observation and interpretation of natural objects—stars and planets—which were creations of God. Astrology observed the given order and did not try to change it. How could you change the course of the stars in the sky or alter the date of a person's birth?

The lingering paganism that really irked Christian clergy was the veneration of nature: worshiping trees and stones, wells and streams. Here Christianity followed Pope Gregory's advice and did its best to replace pagan loci of worship with Christian sites, places where miracles had occurred or saints had been martyred. Although this had good short-term results, there were ramifications centuries in the future that the early medieval proselytizers could hardly have imagined. Just as Christians had condemned the religion that came before them as demonic paganism, Protestants condemned Catholicism as demonic paganism, which had both accommodated too much of ancient paganism in its early years and slipped back into pagan ways of thinking in its later years. The *daimons* had their revenge.

Although Christianity did its best to stamp out the belief in and practice of pagan magic by defining all unsanctioned magic as demonic, it did not eliminate the belief that magical things could and did happen. After all, it was a religion that based its claim to authority on miracles. Christianity merely recategorized the supernatural into signs either of sanctity or of Satanism. Those who performed supernatural feats did not have power in themselves, but became the conduits of the will of God or of the Devil, their acts serving as signs of divine or demonic power.

As the practice of confession and penance became institutionalized, priests found themselves faced with laypeople who confessed to activities that were obviously pagan survivals. Penitentials, handbooks recommending appropriate penance for common sins, began to be written in the sixth century in Ireland and were widespread by the tenth or eleventh century. Throughout Europe, magic that caused death rated a penance of seven years, three of which were to be spent subsisting on bread and water. Love magic, however, only required six months to one year of penance, also on bread and water.

The late seventh century English penitential of Theodore dictated penances for sacrificing to pagan deities (one to ten years, depending on the seriousness of the offense), putting a child in an oven or on the roof to cure a fever (seven years), burning grain after a death to purify the house and its inhabitants (five years), the performance of incantations or divinations by a woman—apparently men did not commit this sin (one year, one or three forty-day periods, depending on the seriousness of the offense), or eating food that has been sacrificed (here the penance was left to the priest to determine according to the specific circumstances). The penitential of Bede, composed a century later, does prescribe penance for a man who practices augury and divination, and also warns against employing "jugglers and chanting diviners" during a lunar eclipse, wearing grass or amber amulets to ward off bad luck, and celebrating the pagan holidays of Thursday and January 1.

A ninth century Spanish penitential warns against consulting fortune tellers, diviners, and enchanters; reading omens in dreams, writing, woolen work, or magic; collecting herbs; or celebrating the first of the month with unspecified customs involving wool. Also forbidden are various rituals involving bathing, sometimes backwards (apparently there was a prescribed order of bathing that could be inverted), men dancing wearing women's clothes, making images, raising storms, or, again, burning grain in a house where a death has occurred. Another ninth century penitential, this one from France, forbids most of the by now common sins—divination and fortune telling, causing harm or love by magic, celebrating New Year's Day with fancy dress and ritual, conjuring storms, making and wearing amulets—as well as making vows by rivers and trees, eating and drinking near pagan sacred places, and eating blood or a dead body that has been offered to pagan idols.

In twelfth century England, these sins are all still cause for concern, as well as magically stealing another's milk or honey, using magic to prevent the consummation of a marriage (presumably by causing the husband to be impotent), and hanging charms in the grass, trees, or at the crossroads to ward off illness from cattle. Several items make specific reference to involvement with pagan deities: throwing a bow into the granary so that "fauns" will increase the harvest, "rid[ing] in the service of her whom the stupid crowd call Herodias or Diana," and laying a table with three knives so that the Fates will bless the inhabitants of the house. It is also forbidden to believe that humans can turn into wolves and that the croaking of crows and ravens or meeting a priest or animal on the road is good or bad luck (the familiar black cat crossing one's path?). In particular, this penitential warns against using the clothing or body of a dead person to make divinations, or to perform rituals to prevent anyone else in the house from dying or to benefit one's own health or advantage (http://www.summerlands.com/crossroads/remembrance/penitent.htm).

The *Decretum* of Burchard of Worms is an eleventh century German penitential written in a chatty style that disturbingly foreshadows 1950s advertising rhetoric:

> Do you believe this, in common with many women who are followers of Satan? Namely, that in the silence of the night, when you are stretched out on your bed with your husband's head on your breast you have the power, flesh as you are, to go out of the closed door and traverse great stretches of space with other women in a similar state of self-deception? (Migne 1878-1890, p. 140).

Have no fear: Forty days of penance for seven consecutive years will have your soul shining like new! Nonetheless, even Burchard and all the penances and punishments of the Catholic Church could not stamp out shamanic soul flight.

CHAPTER 4

MABINOGI, MERLIN, AND MORGAN

PRIOR TO THE FOURTEENTH CENTURY, the Church's position was that pagan practices were evil because magic did not exist, and therefore believing in it was a delusion (miracles were obviously another matter altogether). Those who claimed to be able to see into the future through reading oracles were cheats and cons; medical magic and the use of amulets gave people false security that they could evade God's less delightful plans for them. The sins of paganism enumerated in the penitentials revolved around a few general concepts: the use of incantations and amulets, whether to cause someone harm, create love, cure illness, or ward off bad luck; celebrations of pagan holidays, especially New Years, which involved masking and other forms of disguise as well as feasting on food and drink that had been dedicated to pagan gods; making vows and sacrifices to or by pagan gods and sacred places; pagan death rituals; raising storms; and predicting the future.

Although the similarity between penitentials written four hundred years apart in societies as different and distant as Ireland and Spain suggests that they were copied from each other with relatively little concern for local conditions, the paganism they depict is very much involved with daily life and mundane concerns. People wanted to be happy, safe, and loved, to have fun, and to relieve the anxiety of not knowing what would happen to them. Less well-inclined people wanted to harm others without direct confrontation or exertion. Most of the penitentials assume that these practices are wholly or predominantly the domain of women. It is interesting, however, that while they use words that are usually translatable as "witchcraft" to describe the activities, they do not call their penitents "witches." The phraseology is vague, but it also appears that, unlike with classical witches like Canidia and Erichtho, love magic was not being used by old women to get socially inappropriate sex.

The magic condemned by the penitentials is the kind of thing that Fletcher was referring to as evidence of "country conservatism," time-honored ways of ensuring the beneficence of the supernatural world. It is not, in fact, magic so much as maligned religion. The one area that seems to carry the whiff of the Otherworld is the belief in following Diana in a kind of out-of-body experience. The magic depicted in medieval literature, however, is very much of the Otherworld.

The Otherworld is an ever-present threat or promise in medieval Celtic literature. In Ireland, magic is clearly the realm of the Tuatha Dé Danann, the "tribe of the goddess Danu," who are also known as the *sídhe* or fairy folk. In Irish literature, there is a clear distinction between mundane mortals and the immortal fairies; they are, for all intents and purposes, different races, and with more justification for that classification than the difference between Caucasians and Negroes. Fairies live, for the most part, in another dimension, inhabiting the same space as humans but in a different way, so that they are usually invisible to us. Their world is the opposite of ours, as exemplified in the fact that summer in our world is winter in theirs, and vice versa. They formerly ruled the land; we rule it now. We live on the surface of the earth, while they live within it. We live in the houses of the living, they live in the houses of the dead, the Neolithic burial mounds and fortresses that scatter the face of Ireland. Nonetheless, mortals and fairies can mate and produce fertile offspring, and so many ancient Irish families claim a fairy ancestor or two in their family tree. The magic of Irish fairies lies in their great knowledge, especially their ability to prophesy; their technological expertise, which allows them to create amazing weapons; their musical skills, which traditionally can cause people to weep, laugh, or sleep just by hearing it; their poetry, which can have the effect of a spell, causing that which they speak to occur; their superhuman strength and beauty; their ability to shape-shift, especially between human and animal (or bird) form; and their eternal youth.

Magic in the Welsh tales is less clearly Other and therefore more slippery. There is no distinct race such as the Tuatha Dé, although there are magical families like the family of Dôn (not surprisingly, the Welsh cognate of Danu). The Irish Otherworld is more clearly in, under, or over from here—inside the fairy mound, under the lake, over the sea. The Welsh Otherworld sneaks up on you; one moment you are riding through the woods and the next thing you know you are Somewhere that is definitely Else.

The primary compendium of medieval Welsh mythology is the *Mabinogion* (see Ford, 1977; Jones and Jones, 1948), a collection of eleven tales, including the *Pedeir Ceinc y Mabinogi* or Four Branches of the Mabinogi, as well as five Arthurian tales and two unclassified tales. They are literary compositions, as opposed to oral traditions or explicit myths, but mythic and legendary material is easily discernable within them.

Shape-shifting is endemic; people trade forms with other people, and people turn into animals and birds. In the First Branch, Arawn, the king of Annwfn (the Otherworld; the word means, literally, "not-this-world") tricks Pwyll, the (mortal) prince of Dyfed, into trading places with him so that Pwyll can kill Arawn's enemy Hafgan, who can only be killed with a single blow—an additional blow to polish him off just brings him back to life. In order to disguise the substitution of warriors, Arawn trades shapes with Pwyll; he takes Pwyll's place in Dyfed for a year, while Pwyll takes his in Annwn. In the Third Branch, Manawydan (who has married Pwyll's widow, Rhiannon) saves Dyfed from a magical spell that has laid the land waste by holding hostage the magician's wife, who with her court has taken the form of a mouse in order to steal Manawydan's crops. Llwyd, the magician, takes three different forms to try to trick Manawydan into releasing the mouse: he appears as a scholar, a priest, and a bishop.

The Fourth Branch is the most shape-shifty of all the branches. Gwydion takes on the shape of a bard in order to incite a war with Pryderi. He tricks Pryderi by trading mushrooms transformed into horses and dogs with fancy, jeweled trappings for Pryderi's Otherworldly pigs. Later, Gwydion and Gilfaethwy are punished for a rape by being turned into three different pairs of animals—one male and one female—and produce a set of three human/animals who become famous warriors. Gwydion's sister Arianrhod gives birth to a boy whom she abandons, and Gwydion takes his nephew under his wing. Since Arianrhod curses the boy never to get a name or arms, except from her; Gwydion tricks her into naming the boy Lleu and giving him arms through more shape shifting, and when she adds a final curse that the boy will never get a wife from any race on Earth, Gwydion conjures a wife for him out of flowers. Later, Lleu is killed standing with one foot on the edge of a bathtub and the other on the back of a billy goat, transfixed by a spear constructed only during the time when Mass was being said. He turns into an eagle, and later is turned back into a human (wasted to skin and bone) by Gwydion. Finally, Lleu's faithless wife Blodeuwedd, the woman made from flowers, is transformed yet again, this time into an owl.

The Second Branch adds giants to the mix, along with a magical cauldron. The cauldron is created by the giants Llassar Llaes Gyfnewid and his wife Cymidei Cymeinfoll, and it has the property of returning slain warriors to life, albeit without the ability to speak. Cymidei furthermore has the ability to give birth every six weeks to a boy who will, in another six weeks, become a fully grown warrior. The giant pair were driven out of Ireland because they reproduced so quickly that the Irish felt threatened by them; the Welsh, however, welcomed the pair and solved the baby boom problem by spreading the warriors throughout the land rather than allowing them to accumulate in one place. The architect of this wise policy is Bran the Blessed, himself a giant so large that no house has ever been able to hold him, and who can wade across the Irish Sea with an army of musicians on his back. After being fatally wounded in the heel, Bran commands his companions to cut off his head and take it to Harlech for seven years and the island of Gwales for eighty, during which time the head is as good company dead as it was when Bran was alive.

Although these characters have magic powers, wield magic objects, and live beyond death, they still inhabit their own world. These stories do not draw a line with "us" on one side and "them" (Otherworldly beings) on the other. Arawn's Annwfn seems to occupy the same physical space as Pwyll's Dyfed as a kind of alternate dimension. The Ireland of the Second Branch and the England of the Third are Otherworlds in relation to Wales, while Gwynedd in the Fourth Branch, ruled by a magical king who must keep his feet in the lap of a virgin at all times, except in time of war, seems to be an Otherworld itself. Rhiannon, a magical being who is most probably a euhemerized Celtic goddess (her name means "Divine Queen"), marries the very mortal Pwyll; their son Pryderi, therefore, is half mortal and half Otherworldly. After Pwyll's death, Rhiannon marries Manawydan, another euhemerized deity.

While the Four Branches of the Mabinogi are unique to Welsh literature, the Welsh Arthurian romances form a bridge between Celtic mythology and the broader range of medieval European literature. Magical objects are even more important in the Arthurian literature than in the Mabinogi—the earliest extant Welsh Arthurian story, *Culhwch and Olwen*, is essentially a serial quest for the magical objects necessary for the giant Ysbaddaden Pencawr to groom himself and prepare the wedding feast for his daughter Olwen's marriage to the hero Culhwch.

Of course, since it is prophesied that Ysbaddaden will die when his daughter marries, the quests are difficult, if not impossible, and Culhwch has to enlist the aid of his cousin Arthur. This is a story that loves lists—the plot screeches to a halt as the narrator enumerates every warrior and lady of Arthur's court, a list that goes on for nine manuscript columns and comprises some 260 names—and Ysbaddaden makes forty demands that must be fulfilled before the wedding can take place. Many, however, are prerequisites for the next step of the quest (in order to hunt the magical boar Twrch Trwyth, who holds the razor and scissors to groom Ysbaddaden's hair between his two ears, special dogs must be obtained, along with magical collars and leashes, magical warriors to hold the leashes, more magical warriors to ride to the hunt on magical horses, and a magical sword to kill the boar once he is caught).

In the romance of Owein son of Urien Rheged, the maiden Luned gives the hero a magical ring that makes him invisible when he turns the stone to the inside of his hand. This ring is one of the "Thirteen Treasures of the Island of Britain" (Bromwich 1978, pp. 240-249). The other treasures are the Sword of Rhydderch Hael, the Hamper of Gwyddno Garanhir, the Horn of Bran Galed, the Chariot of Morgan Mwynfawr, the Halter of Clydno Eiddyn, the Knife of Llawfrodedd Farchog, the Cauldron of Diwrnach Gawr, the Whetstone of Tudwal Tudglyd, the Coat of Padarn Beisrydd, the Crock and Dish of Rhygenydd Ysgolhaig, the Chessboard of Gwenddolau ap Ceidio, the Mantle of Arthur, and the Mantle of Tegau Eurvron, as well as the Stone and Ring of Luned.

These treasures are similar to the type of magical objects demanded by Ysbaddaden—in fact, Diwrnach's cauldron is one of them, and reference is also made to Gwyddno's hamper in *Culhwch and Olwen*. Many of the objects are involved in the magical production of food, while others, such as the chariot and halter, provide magical transportation. Gwenddolau's chessboard, on which the pieces move by themselves, is similar to the chessboard on which Arthur and Owein play in *The Dream of Rhonabwy*. Several objects have different qualities according to the person who uses them: Padarn's coat would be the right size for any nobleman who wore it, but a peasant could not even get it on; Tegau's mantle would reach the ground when worn by a chaste woman, but reach only the lap of an adulteress. Arthur's mantle, like Luned's ring, conferred invisibility. Yet while the objects are magical, the people who own them are not; with the exception of Diwrnach, who is a giant, all are normal, if exceptional, mortals.

The theme of shape-shifting is somewhat attenuated in the Welsh romances. The closest is Owein's fate, when his Otherworldly bride repudiates him for his abandonment of her; he wanders for years with the animals of the woods until he becomes covered with long hair. Eventually he stumbles back into civilization, where he is healed with a magical ointment that causes the hair to fall off. This seems to be a watered-down version of the punishment meted out to Gwydion and Gilfaethwy, who are turned into real animals by means of Math's magic wand. The romance of Owein also includes a giant who is Master of the Animals, a magical fountain, the supernatural birds of Rhiannon, a very friendly lion, and a monstrous *bwystfil* who eats people. The romance of Gereint is adventurous—much jousting, brawling, and general mayhem—but light on real magic. Only at the end of the tale does the hero encounter enchanted games held within a magical hedge of mist (the druids were said to be able to conjure such mists). Like the fountain in the romance of Owein, where casting the fountain's water upon a rock summons a supernatural opponent, the mist (atmospheric water) encloses a throne, sitting upon which constitutes a challenge to the resident champion. After Gereint defeats his opponent, he sounds a magical horn that disperses the mist and puts an end to the deadly games.

In the romance of Peredur, we finally encounter witches. The story tells of the education and coming-of-age of a naive youth who has been raised far from the court so that he will never learn how to joust—the occupation that killed his father. About halfway through his adventures, Peredur encounters the nine witches of Caer Loyw, i.e., Gloucester. Although these witches appear to be of evil intent, killing every human they encounter and laying waste to the countryside, they are also prophesied to train Peredur in battle and to give him horse and arms. In this they are similar to the Otherworldly warrior woman Scathach, who trains the Irish hero Cú Chulainn, and perhaps also to the warrior queen Medb and the triple Irish war goddess Morrígan. It is interesting, however, that the word used for these "witches" is *gwrach*, which is the common Welsh word for a witch, but really just means "old woman." It is also the name given to a kind of wasting fever, which no doubt was once thought to have a supernatural origin.

The romance of Peredur also contains the most magical object of all medieval literature, the Grail. However, unlike Chrétien de Troyes's romance of Percival, where the Grail is some kind of chalice or platter, or the later continuations of Chrétien in which the Grail is the cup of the Last Supper, an object with a direct connection to Jesus, in Peredur, the "grail" is a platter holding a man's bloody severed head. Severed heads are very magical objects in Celtic literature; like Bran the Blessed's head, they often continue talking after death. Peredur also encounters a monster called an Addanc, which lives in a cave and throws poisoned stone spears at his attackers; elsewhere in Welsh folklore the Addanc is a kind of ferocious beaver that pulls people down into a lake, where they drown. Peredur overcomes the Addanc with the help of yet another stone of invisibility. On his way to the Addanc's cave he sees wonders such as a river with a flock of white sheep on one side and black sheep on the other, and if a sheep crosses from one side to the other, its color changes accordingly. There is also a tree that is green on one side and on fire on the other. There is even some shape-shifting in the person of Peredur's cousin, who appears in the forms of several different women, one of them so hideous she takes a whole paragraph to describe, and also in the form of a young man. Peredur comes across a Castle of Wonders that contains yet another self-playing chessboard, and there he kills his former teachers, the witches of Caer Loyw, who are still in their killing ways. Although the romance of Peredur is a very fractured and disjointed narrative, it is also a grab-bag of Celtic mythological and magical motifs.

Versions of the Arthurian legends were told in all the major languages of medieval Europe, as well as several of the more obscure ones, and there is much cross-pollination between tales in different languages. Although Arthur makes his earliest appearances in Welsh legend, especially in saints' lives, the Welsh Arthurian tales show evidence of both unique native tradition and fashionable Continental motifs. Yet one of the distinguishing characteristics of Arthurian literature in any language—as in the medieval Welsh and Irish prose narratives, Arthurian and otherwise—is the prevalence of magic and the Otherworld as more than a simple plot device. The primary magician of the Arthurian world is the wizard Merlin; his primary opponent in the magic game is Morgan le Fay. Once again, there is a contrast between good male magic and bad female magic.

The real contrast, however, is between classical literary magic and medieval literary magic. The witches evoked by Horace, Lucan, Apollonius, and Euripides are normal humans who have gone bad and who command magic by invoking goddesses and other supernatural beings through spells and incantations. Medieval magic is generally performed by individuals who are magical in and of themselves. They don't have to invoke goddesses because, many would argue, they are goddesses, demoted to an intermediate space between deity and human—the daimonic realm.

Neither Morgan nor Merlin appear in the native Welsh Arthurian romances, but Merlin—the native form of his name, Myrddin—is a significant figure. The list of the Names of the Island of Britain (Bromwich 1978, pp. 228-229) also notes that the first name of the island, before it was settled by humans, was Clas Myrddin, "Myrddin's Precinct." In the early tenth century prophetic poem *Armes Prydein*, one stanza begins with the words "Myrddin foretells," paralleling the opening of other stanzas, "Awen [poetic inspiration] foretells" and "Druids foretell." This would seem to suggest that Myrddin is interchangeable with both priests and poets.

Myrddin appears in Triad 87 as one—or possibly two—of the Three Skillful Bards of Arthur's Court (Bromwich 1978, p. 214): Myrddin son of Morfryn, Myrddin Emrys, and Taliesin. Bromwich notes a sixteenth century tradition that Myrddin Emrys had been reincarnated as Taliesin and then as Myrddin son of Morfryn, also known as Myrddin Wyllt, "Myrddin the insane."

However, the pre-twelfth century poem "Conversation between Myrddin and Taliesin" shows that at that time, the two were considered to be distinct, and contemporary, characters. Taliesin himself is believed to have flourished in the second half of the sixth century in the court of Urien Rheged, a king whose realm straddled the western half of Hadrian's Wall. Both A. O. H. Jarman (1978) and Nikolai Tolstoy (1985) have argued that the figure of Myrddin Wyllt overlaps with and in some cases may be identical to Lailoken, a mad prophet in the hagiography of St. Kentigern (c. 518-603), and Suibhne Geilt ("Mad Sweeney"), a legendary Irish king of the Dal Araidhe, the people of northern Ireland who colonized the area of western Scotland that came to be known as Dalriada. He was supposed to have gone mad during the same Battle of Magh Rath, c. 634, in which Cennfaeladh lost his brain of forgetting. Myrddin himself is supposed to have gone insane during the Battle of Arderydd, c. 573, and then to have lived in the woods of southwestern Scotland, where he prophesied and composed poetry. Myrddin, then, is part of a fragmented myth or legend of some kind of battle-crazed poet-prophet of what is now southwestern Scotland some time between 550 and 650.

This early, quasihistorical Myrddin is, like Canidia, Erichtho, and Medea, a mortal with one foot in the mortal realm and the other in the Otherworld. However, by the time he shows up in Geoffrey of Monmouth's *Historia Regum Britanniae* in the early twelfth century, he has become a sage and sane counselor, a powerful, shape-shifting wizard, and a demon/human hybrid, the son of a princess and the Devil. (Indeed, Geoffrey's description of Merlin's father explicitly identifies him as a classic daimon, with reference to Apuleius.) However, Merlin is also contrasted with Vortigern's mere "magicians," who have decreed that the blood of a fatherless boy will still the earth tremors that have been destroying the foundation of the king's mountain fortress; only Merlin can correctly predict that the real culprits are restless dragons within the earth. Geoffrey then makes a long aside in his text to relate Merlin's political prophecies, including the death of Vortigern.

Merlin next appears to advise Aurelius Ambrosius to bring the "Giant's Dance," a megalithic circle, from "Killaraus" (possibly Kilkenny), Ireland, to Salisbury Plain to memorialize Britons treacherously slain by the Saxons. This, of course, refers to Stonehenge. Merlin alone is able to devise the equipment necessary to take down the stones and transport them first to ships and then to their destination in Britain. Merlin's renowned transformation of Uther Pendragon into the semblance of Gorlois, Duke of Cornwall, in order to satisfy his lust for Igerna, is accomplished by means of "medicines." He does not, contrary to later tradition, have any part in the reign of Arthur himself; Arthur is advised by a college of one hundred philosophers, who prophesy for him. Merlin's talents, then, according to Geoffrey, are prophecy, mechanical and technological wizardry, and the making of magical potions. The source of his wisdom is not explicitly identified, but it appears to derive from Otherworldly insight inherited from his daimonic father.

In the *Historia Regum Britanniae*, Modred, Arthur's killer, is his nephew, son of Arthur's sister Anne and her husband Lot. Morgan le Fay does not appear at all. However, Morgan does show up in Geoffrey's follow-up to the *Historia*, his *Vita Merlini*. This book was evidently written to account for additional material on Merlin that Geoffrey had discovered after completing the earlier book, and it appears to be based on the legends of the northern, mad Myrddin rather than the southern sage.

Morgen (as her name is spelled in this text) turns up in a section consisting of a conversation between Merlin and "Telgesinus" or Taliesin. Telgesinus is delivering a lecture to the mad Merlin, imparting information about the nature of wind and rainstorms—and also mentioning the Neoplatonic doctrine of daimons dwelling in the region between the moon and Earth—wandering off into a discussion of the nature of the ocean, its fishy inhabitants, and culminating with a brief gazetteer of the more interesting islands in that ocean. Among these is the "Island of Apples" or "Fortunate Island," where crops sprout and orchards fruit spontaneously and men live to be one hundred years old. Nine sisters rule this island, and the chief sister, most beautiful and most skilled in healing and astrology, is Morgen. She also can change her shape, sprout wings, and fly wherever she chooses. There, Telgesinus says, is where they took Arthur to heal his wounds after the Battle of Camlann; Morgen, after assessing the extent of his injury, said that the king would heal, but only if he were left with her for an extended course of treatment.

Basil Clarke, translator of the *Vita Merlini* (1973), notes that Morgen *per se*, and especially her role as Arthur's healer, appears to be Geoffrey's invention. He identifies the underlying structure of this episode as an Arthurization of the story of Circe and Odysseus: "an island queen of magical powers receiving a royal hero" (Clarke 1973, p. 203). The motif of the nine magical, island-dwelling maidens may be a reference to Pomponius Mela's first century C.E. description of nine virgins who lived on an island that was probably one of the Scilly Isles; they could raise storms, shape-shift, heal, and prophesy. The spelling "Morgen" suggests that the etymology of her name may be *môr-geni*, "born of the sea," although this is the subject of some debate. In addition to Geoffrey's Morgen, there are references to a "nymph" Morgan, who is Arthur's sister and who made him immortal, in a Breton romance, *Draco Nomanicus*, written in 1168, and in the mid-twelfth century Welsh Arthurian romance *Gereint vab Erbin* Arthur's (male) physician is named Morgan Tud.

Morgan acquires her popular character of a powerful sorceress opposed to Arthur and his court in *Sir Gawain and the Green Knight*, a late fourteenth century Middle English romance in alliterative verse. After Gawain has proven his valor by showing himself willing to allow the Green Knight to cut off his head, the knight explains all:

> Bernlak de Hautdesert am I called in this land. Morgain le Fay dwelleth in mine house, and through knowledge of clerkly craft hath she taken many. For long time was she the mistress of Merlin, who knew well all you knights of the court. Morgain the goddess is she called therefore, and there is none so haughty but she can bring him low. She sent me in this guise to yon fair hall to test the truth of the renown that is spread abroad of the valour of the Round Table. She taught me this marvel to betray your wits, to vex Guinevere and fright her to death by the man who spake with his head in his hand at the high table. That is she who is at home, that ancient lady, she is even thine aunt, Arthur's half-sister, the daughter of the Duchess of Tintagel, who afterward married King Uther. (Jessie Weston, trans. http://www.lib.rochester.edu/CAMELOT/sggk.htm)

Morgan is now both Arthur's half-sister and Merlin's student, and her magic drives from "clerkly craft," that is, book-learning. This would seem to downgrade Morgan's power—she has learned male, literary magic and she has turned it to malicious female purpose in a catty attempt to frighten Guinevere. Yet she is also known as "Morgain the goddess," hinting that her magic is indeed something innate.

Morgan attains her most unpleasant characteristics in the French Vulgate cycle. She is said to be the wife of King Uriens and thus the mother of Yvain, the French form of Owein, and is possibly also the mother of Gawain, and/or Mordred. Morgan's enmity toward Guinevere is explained in the Prose *Lancelot*, in which her affair with Guinevere's cousin is put to an end by the queen. She attempts, unsuccessfully, to seduce Lancelot in retaliation against Guinevere, and tries to expose Lancelot and Guinevere's affair when she fails. She seduces Merlin in order to learn the magic she needs for her nefarious schemes. Here we can see that Morgan's magic has segued from being beneficent and healing—in Chrétien's *Yvain* the ointment that heals the mad and hairy hero is her concoction, and another of her ointments heals the hero of *Erec et Enide*—to being self-centered and focused on her own sexual gratification. In the Prose *Tristan*, however, Morgan uses her healing and harming powers in a ploy to seduce the young knight Alisander Orphelin. Her modus operandi has turned from mystical knowledge to the use of date-rape drugs.

The contrast between Merlin and Morgan develops into a contrast between good and bad magic, with the attendant ascription of good and bad to the male and female, respectively. Over the course of her medieval history, Morgan changes from a supernatural, benevolent, healing figure to a mortal, wicked, sexually rapacious, death-dealing figure: She changes from a goddess to a witch. Merlin, for his part, remains fairly stable in his character. While some texts might emphasize his statesmanlike wisdom while others feature his foolishness in love, he is always a good guy, and his knowledge is always valuable and socially constructive. It is when his knowledge falls into the hands of a woman—whether she be Morgan, Vivian, Nimue—that it is put to evil purposes. This would imply that magic itself is morally neutral, and its good or bad effects result from the intent of the magician.

However, statistically, women are represented as being more "magical" than men in medieval literature; magic is represented as naturally part of the female domain, and therefore it is always potentially tainted, because women are shown always to use it selfishly. Furthermore, the women who use magic are human, mortal. The power and talent of the great male magician, Merlin, is ascribed to his half-demonic nature. He is not a mere mortal; from the very beginning, he has one foot in the Otherworld.

Nonetheless, the magic that appears in medieval literature—and not just in the Celtic and Celtic-inspired texts analyzed here—is either innate, due to an individual's nature, or it is the result of learning, whether oral or literary. It is not a power acquired by selling one's soul to the Devil, making a Satanic pact, or through the worship of demons or goddesses such as Hecate. The Irish and Welsh tales are presented as tales of the pre-Christian past, with direct reference at points to the fact that the people of Ireland and Wales had a different religion in the past. Some of the magic in them is dismissed through authorial commentary on the grounds that, while it was the result of demonic action, prior to Christianity, no one knew any better. Yet the magic, even if performed as the result of demonic interference in the world, is not something that people deliberately incite the demons to produce. By the time of the later Arthurian romances, there is no longer even a hint of underlying paganism. Morgan may be evil, but she operates purely within a Christian context (and in some cases is said to have learned her magic in a convent).

There appears to be no connection made between religion and magic in these tales. Celtic scholars commonly ascribe the lack of direct reference to the rituals of pagan religion in the medieval tales to monkish censorship. The monks, it is argued, wanted to preserve the tales, but did not want to glorify or promote paganism, and therefore glossed over whatever explicit religion had been in the tales originally. However, this explanation inadvertently glosses over the fact that the monks might well have decided to combat the paganism in the tales with aggressive rather than passing commentary on its demonic origin.

Indeed, magic as something that can be learned from books makes magic something that clerics, the only section of society in which literacy was routine rather than exceptional, might well practice. The word "grimoire," after all—grimoire being a book of rituals, recipes, spells, and other magical information hand-copied by one witch from another—is derived from "grammar," as is "glamour." Scholarship had the potential to be magical. However, this kind of scholarship, the domain of males, is presented as benevolent in the hands of men in the narratives. At a time when there was serious debate about whether women had souls and whether it was a wise thing to teach them to read, it is no wonder that fictional women who got their hands on scholarly magic tended to use it badly. Good female magic was confined to healing, an area in which female proficiency derived from oral tradition rather than book learning.

It is odd, however, that in an era when the Church's official position on magic was that those who claimed to practice it were delusional rather than heretical, there is so much literature imbued with magic, and magic of an almost mundane quality. Not that the effects of the magic were mundane, but that magic was something humanly acquired and practiced. Magical power is presented as being innate in some people, whether because of an Otherworldly ancestor somewhere, near or far, in the family tree, because of either innate wisdom or scholarly learning, or simply just because. The world of medieval fiction, especially Arthurian fiction, is a world in which weird stuff just happens all the time. It is completely possible for people to change shape, becoming either an animal or a different human. While ordinary tools, like food hampers, cauldrons, or goblets, might facilitate the production and consumption of food, it is completely possible for there to be tools that make the production and consumption of food no work at all. It's hard to walk all the way to the next town; it's easier to get there riding on horseback; but just imagine if there were a chariot that would get you there in the blink of an eye!

These are mundane, not theological, concerns. They show up in fictional tales to lend glamour, in the original sense of the word. Just as the people in movies always live in much nicer houses than real people of their social class and income do, the characters in medieval romances had much more powerful weapons, cutlery, clothing, and transportation than real knights did.

The fictional magical world was very different from the magic practiced in real life in the medieval world. Yes, Morgan le Fay might create healing ointments in Chrétien's romances, but she, and other characters in those romances, did not pass ailing babies through a split tree-trunk and leave bits of their clothes tied to bramble bushes. She did not leave her body in bed and ride with Diana in spirit. She was very rarely even called a witch. The one point where real and literary magic overlap is in the belief that women use magic for unfair or unnatural sexual advantages. Magic, in male hands, is scholarship; in female hands, it is sex.

CHAPTER 5

BURN HER

THE PERIOD OF THE EUROPEAN WITCH HUNTS has been analyzed within an inch of its life over the past hundred years. One reason is, ironically, the rise of anthropology as an academic discipline. As Europeans spread across the world in waves of imperialism, beginning with the discovery of the Americas at the end of the fifteenth century, they encountered peoples of very different cultures, religions, social organizations, and skin colors. Initially, European explorers, merchants, and missionaries contented themselves with documenting the outlandish behavior and beliefs of these Others, yet as the European mindset became increasingly oriented toward science, with its interest in classification, categorization, and experimentation, scholars began to formulate theories about the relationships between human groups.

One self-evident question was, why were the Europeans colonizing and economically exploiting the Americas, Asians, and Africans, and not vice versa? What made Europeans different? One answer was that they were, in some way, better, whether because of the color of their skin, the rightness of their religion, the efficiency of their economic system, or the sophistication of their social organization. (Or all of the above.) Out of the goodness of their hearts, therefore, Europeans did their best to remedy the deficiencies in the rest of the world's religion, economy, and social organization (although there was, sadly, nothing to be done about skin color). Nonetheless, there were some disturbing similarities, they discovered, between the lives of these "savages" and "primitives" and certain aspects of European life in the not-too-distant past.

Charles Darwin's theory of evolution by natural selection, first set forth in his *On the Origin of Species* (1859), was only intended to apply to the physical evolution of animals and plants, but even though it was greeted with horror and disgust by many, who were appalled at the idea of being descended from apes, those who did embrace evolutionary theory in the second half of the nineteenth century did so with gusto. Social theorists, especially anthropologists, expanded the idea of evolution from the physical to the psychological and the social, propounding what came to be called Social Darwinism. This handily explained why European society was overrunning the rest of the world: it was more "fit." Social evolution was conceived as a ladder, with monotheistic, capitalist, European society at its pinnacle and the rest of the world in a strict hierarchy below it. But European society had not always been so superior, not any more than humans had been created ex nihilo by God; just as humans had evolved from apes, who were still around to illustrate mankind's previous state, so European society had evolved from more primitive forms of society, which were still around as well.

Furthermore, illustrating Ernst Haeckel's 1866 dictum that "ontogeny recapitulates phylogeny" (i.e., that the physical development of an individual goes through all the evolutionary steps experienced by its species, but faster, and usually in the womb), European children's social development recapitulated the stages of primitive society. Thus, the non-European "savage" and the European child were intellectual and social peers. Equally, the "less advanced" strata of European society—the peasants or, as they were increasingly called during the nineteenth century, the folk—were equivalent to perhaps the middle years of childhood socialization in their intellectual sophistication. Anthropologists as a general rule studied the Other abroad, while folklorists studied the Other at home.

One point of contact that made it possible to envision a continuum of human social evolution, from the primitive (archetypally African or Native American, and always of a tribal social organization) to the folk (rural European peasants conceived as living essentially the same lifestyle since the Middle Ages) was witchcraft. In the eyes of early twentieth century anthropologists and folklorists, the witch hunts of the early modern era—roughly 1500 to 1700—marked the last spasm of European primitivism, and their cessation marked the beginning of the Age of Reason, when Europeans entered the home stretch in their race to world social and moral superiority (an attitude that has substantially altered in the last fifty years). It may be no coincidence that this last era of European primitivism (in its own eyes) coincided with the discovery of new, improved, and more exciting primitives elsewhere in the world.

Explanations for the witch hunts have ranged from the discovery of hitherto unsuspected pagan survivals to uncontrollable misogyny, to anxiety aroused by the breakdown of traditional village society, to displaced religious fervor created by the Reformation. A good argument can be made for each. Carlo Ginzburg's research on the *benandanti* and related, mostly Eastern European, folk religions has shown that remnants of shamanism lingered on in Europe into the early modern period and were reinterpreted by elite theology as Satanism; however, Margaret Murray's theory that a strictly organized paganism lingered, unsuspected by the Church, is unlikely. Women certainly constituted the larger percentage of accused and executed witches; in the most extreme cases, all but a handful of the women living in some small villages were executed (although men were also accused and executed).

In addition to being female, many of the accused were marginal members of society who had formerly been cared for within tight-knit communities, but who were falling between the cracks as feudal, agricultural society began to reorient itself into urban, mercantile society. Accused witches were usually old and poor, and had often been refused alms or other assistance by those who claimed to be under magical attack. It seems almost elementary psychology that their own parsimony and lack of compassion would lead people to displace their guilt onto those who occasioned it; a classic case of blaming the victim.

However, while many witches were of low and marginal social status compared to their accusers, the low also accused the high and mighty—although one of the factors that seems to have halted witch crazes was when too many socially prominent people began to be named in confessions. The period of the witch hunts does coincide with the Reformation, and one of the strategies used by both Catholics and Protestants was to demonize the religious practices of the other side—a tactic literalized in witchcraft accusations. On the scale of broad generalization, it seems that witch hunts were most common in areas that were not predominantly either Catholic or Protestant, but rather in places where the numbers of each persuasion were closer to equal. Religion, then, tended to be a problematic and unsettled issue in places where witch hunts occurred, but witch hunts did not invariably arise in every place where Catholic-Protestant tensions existed.

During the peak of the witch hunts, conservative estimates suggest that approximately 30,000 people were executed for witchcraft, of whom "three of every four witches executed in Europe between 1560 and 1660 spoke some dialect of German, while six of every seven lived—and died—within the boundaries of the pre-1648 Holy Roman Empire, a region holding about 20% of Europe's population" (Monter 2002, p. 16); the population of Europe has been estimated at around 100 million in 1600, the midpoint of this era. (In comparison, the population of Europe in 2003 was approximately 723 million.) This is considerably less than the 9 million executions claimed by the more extreme estimates, but it is still a considerable number of people to have been killed for something they almost certainly did not do—sell their souls to and worship Satan. Furthermore, as the enormous bias in numbers toward the Germanic world shows, some areas were much harder hit than others.

In the early centuries of Christianity, the Church was concerned with combating the actual paganism that had preceded it. The population of Europe believed in a multiplicity of gods, not only from region to region, but also within local pantheons; Christianity's agenda was to persuade people to accept a single god. On the western edge of Europe, Iceland was the last area to become Christian, in 1000; in the east, Lithuania was the last hold-out, finally converting for good in 1385. By and large, however, Europe could be regarded as a Christian continent by the time of the Crusades, from 1095, when the First Crusade began, to the fall of Acre in 1291.

Roughly, then, Christianity defined itself in contrast to paganism between the early fourth century, when it became the religion of the declining Roman Empire, and the eleventh century, by which time most of Europe was Christian; from the eleventh to the thirteenth century, Christianity defined itself in contrast to Islam. Christianity won over paganism, but it was driven out of the Middle East by Islam; this defeat may have raised some unconscious worries as to how secure the earlier success had really been. In any case, after nearly a millennium of expansion, the failure in the Holy Land was a slap in the face to the Catholic Church.

The Church's attitude toward witchcraft and magic in the early Middle Ages was dismissive; folk beliefs about night flights to follow a pagan goddess, battles for the fertility of the fields, magical healing, cursing, and divination, were the products of deluded minds. Similarly deluded were heretics of various stripes: Cathars, Waldensians, Albigensians. All had to be convinced to change their minds and accept the truth, at the point of a sword if necessary. During the era of the Crusades, however, the fear of organized conspiracies against Christianity began to arise.

Among the first victims of these conspiracy theories were lepers, Jews, and the Knights Templar. Lepers and Jews were suspected of poisoning wells in order to kill all healthy Christians and gain power over the world for themselves. In 1321, this "conspiracy" came to light in France, with the result that many lepers were tortured and burned at the stake. Jews were forced to convert or were lynched; throughout the Middle Ages, they were assumed to be working actively against Christianity by the simple fact of their being Jews (Ginzburg 1991, pp. 33-62). The Knights Templar, who had formed in 1118 to protect pilgrims to the Holy Land during the Second Crusade, were accused in 1307, also in France, of practicing a kind of anti-Christianity that included worshiping an idol named Baphomet, denying Christ, and trampling the Cross, and the Order was disbanded and its members—or those who could be caught—tortured and burned at the stake.

Throughout the late medieval and early modern periods, an increasingly wide gap opened between elite and folk beliefs about witches and what they did. The folk continued to believe, as they always had, that there were people who were capable of using magic to find lost objects, stolen goods, buried treasure, and missing people; to heal sick livestock and humans; to influence the course of love, whether to create it or quell it; to see the future; and to diagnose the actions of other magicians and, if they detected maleficent magic aimed at their clients, to counteract it. These activities were carried out by gazing into mirrors, pools of water, or crystal balls; manipulating a sieve and scissors or key and book; analyzing the bodily fluids or measuring the bodies of the ailing; casting lots; interpreting natural phenomena such as eclipses, earthquakes, or the positions of the stars; speaking with spirits or the dead; and by conjuring spells over crops and people (Clark 2002, pp. 103, 107). They concocted potions that may have had authentic medicinal value, or whose properties were purely psychosomatic.

In large part, however, they used words: spells and incantations spoken in gibberish, decayed Latin, or the straight vernacular. Their books and pieces of paper or metal on which they had inscribed words had magical power in themselves, beyond the mere meaning of the words. This attitude toward the magic power of the written word can be traced back to the *defixiones* of antiquity.

These practitioners of magic had numerous names and, often, specific areas of expertise. Stuart Clark lists some of them (Clark 2002, p. 103): in Italy, magical healers were known as *benandanti, pauliani* (specializing in snakebites), *ciarliatani* (from whence comes the word "charlatan"), *janare, magare,* and *fattucchare*. Hungary had the *táltos* (a healer, treasure-finder, fortune-teller, and defender against witchcraft), *néző* (seer), *tudományos* (wise man), and *javasszony* (soothsayer). In France, there were *devins, conjureurs,* and *leveurs de sorts*. England had cunning men and women, while Wales had *dynion hysbys*. Even when there were no terminological distinctions made between types of magicians, an individual might have one special talent, such as finding treasure or healing cows, for which they were known.

Some of these people participated in elaborate rituals with shamanic overtones, such as the *benandanti*. They were often marked as special from birth, usually by being born with a caul, or teeth, or hair. The source of their power was innate, although they might refine it through apprenticeship with another magician, and if they were pressed to identify a source, they would more often than not say that it came to them from God. They believed that their souls traveled from their bodies in order to do spiritual battle with the forces of evil—forces that were invariably called, by them, "witches." These people were real, whatever one may think of the reality of their powers. They had a defined social role in village life, and their skills were valued, if sometimes feared, by their neighbors.

In contrast, the witches whom they battled or counteracted were largely beings of the spirit world. They were the personification—or anthropomorphization—of everything evil, malevolent, dangerous, or inexplicable in the world. Witches were believed to engage in a variety of acts, but their combined effect can be summarized as stealing fertility. Witches stole, killed, and ate children; blighted crops; made men impotent and made women miscarry; made cows go dry and butter fail to come in the churn; prevented beer from fermenting; called down hail and storms that both ruined harvests and sank ships; they were the source of all illness and most death. In many cases, witches didn't just cause misfortune to others, but also prospered at the expense of their neighbors. If the butter didn't come in your churn, the witch was getting double the butter in hers. If your crops failed, his or hers showed an exceptional yield. One of the ways that a witch could gain power over your household and agricultural activities was to borrow something, and so a way to avoid being cursed was to avoid lending things out, and if you did do so and suffered a run of ill luck, you had to get the item back from the witch.

Witches could change shape in order to carry out their nefarious deeds, becoming wolves, mice, flies, cats, or birds, and if they were injured while in that form, the wound would also appear on their human body once they shifted back. One of the most common witch stories throughout Europe and indeed the whole world is of a person who shoots an animal attacking a flock and then discovers, either then and there or the next morning, that a neighbor or even a relative has exactly the same wound.

From the point of view of the educated and the Church, there was only one type of magical practitioner—the witch—and only one source of its power—the Devil. The power was obtained by selling one's soul to Satan, sometimes through an oral agreement and sometimes through a written contract, and the bargain was sealed by kissing the Devil's anus or engaging in sexual intercourse with him. Witches gathered by smearing their bodies with an ointment that allowed them to fly, or by flying on demons in the shapes of animals such as goats, rams, dogs, or, occasionally, on brooms; in many areas there was a specific place, usually a mountaintop, cave, or forest—in other words, an area outside of the normal realm of human habitation—where their sabbaths were said to occur. There the witches feasted, danced, and had orgies with the Devil. The size of the gathering was variable; the idea that witches gathered in "covens" of thirteen occurs in only a few sources, mostly Scottish, and the insistence of inquisitors that accused witches name their cohorts put no upper limit on the number of witches who might be active in any one area at a time. The Devil called the names of all the attendant witches, and they might respond by listing all their evil activities since the last gathering; the convened group might then sacrifice unbaptized babies, whose roasted flesh formed part of the feast.

Although there was no evil act that witches might not commit, as far as the Church was concerned, witches were not concerned with the theft and destruction of fertility so much as with undermining and overthrowing Christianity. The opportunity to commit evil acts was merely the bait with which Satan lured his followers. The true goal of witchcraft was to replace the Christian congregation with a demonic "synagogue." The adoption of the words "synagogue" and "sabbat" to describe witchy gatherings may, in fact, have been a deliberate choice to conflate the witches' agenda with that of the Jews, who were also believed, by their very nature as Jews, to be dedicated to the overthrow of Christianity.

The fourteenth and fifteenth century saw an increase in the use of accusations of witchcraft and sorcery as means of political manipulation. These accusations were primarily located in the princely courts of continental Europe, not in its villages. This political use of magic was indeed an aspect of conspiracy; in the struggle for power, anything that might get results was fair game, whether the attempt to use magic oneself or accusations of magic use to discredit one's opponents. However, these were human conspiracies, and their aim was to acquire political power from princes as well as from prelates—clerics were often accused of using sorcery, since their literacy was often regarded as close to magical itself, and certainly gave them access to arcane knowledge. The idea that witchcraft was itself a conspiracy dedicated to the overthrow of Christianity, a conspiracy headed by Satan himself, was not part of these witchcraft accusations and trials.

The earliest witchcraft trials that included elements of night flights to witches' gatherings involving worship of Satan, blasphemy, feasting, and sexual perversity as well as the acquisition of power, also began in the early fourteenth century, within fifty years of the end of the Crusades. Of course, at the time, no one could say with certainty that the Crusades were definitively over; however, the beginning of an obsession with witchcraft can be seen as the beginning of a shift in focus from an Enemy Without—Islam—to an Enemy Within—lepers, Jews, but most of all witches.

The trial of Lady Alice Kyteler in Kilkenny, Ireland, in 1324, was the first to include accusations that an organized band of witches met at night to acquire magical power through sexual intercourse with the Devil, and the first in which a woman (not Lady Alice but her maid Petronilla) was tortured and burned at the stake on charges of practicing witchcraft, i.e., worshiping Satan, rather than on charges of subscribing to a Christian heresy, i.e., worshiping God, but in the wrong way. The accusations and trial themselves, however, appear to have had their origin in the same kind of political intrigue that produced witchcraft accusations on the Continent—indeed, Lady Alice's accuser, Richard Ledrede, the bishop of Ossary, had been trained in France.

The fourteenth century was marked by a large number of disasters, natural and human. There was a major famine in 1315-1317, the Black Death struck in 1348-1349 and continued intermittently through 1450, and the Hundred Years War between England and France disrupted international relations from 1337 to 1453. The social turmoil created by these three drains on the population of Europe led to numerous peasant uprisings and the decline of the feudal system. Additionally, in 1308 Pope Clement V moved the court of the papacy from Rome to Avignon, France, and the focus of papal power remained there until 1378, throughout the reigns of seven successive popes. In 1378, the papacy splintered in the Great Schism, during which there were two popes, one based in Avignon and one in Rome, until 1423. This entire state of affairs was viewed by many as indicating an all-too-political intrusion of worldly affairs into the realm of religion, and many felt that the general disasters of the fourteenth century were a heavenly commentary on the corruption of Catholicism.

Medieval Europe had imagined itself a monolithic, as well as a monotheistic, religious community, and the events of the fourteenth and fifteenth centuries forced the realization that it was not. The logical response was to root out these sources of fragmentation and force them into conformity with dogma. Between 1435 and 1500, the stereotype of the female, night-riding, Satan-worshiping witch solidified, abetted by the Church's inclusion of sorcery in its list of heresies in 1320, and a series of papal bulls issued between 1473 and 1484 reemphasizing the heretical nature of sorcery and placing its prosecution under the authority of the Inquisition.

This stereotype was initially held by the educated classes and had little correspondence to folk beliefs about what witches were and what they did. The classic expression of the stereotype of the diabolical witch was the *Malleus Maleficarum*, published in 1487 by Heinrich Kramer, a Swiss Dominican inquisitor, and Jakob Sprenger, another Dominican inquisitor from Cologne. (Although the two are paired as coauthors of the work, the extent of Sprenger's involvement has become open to question.) Kramer was well known for his personal misogyny, and his obsession with questioning the women who came before him on their sexual lives caused his fellow inquisitors acute discomfort and indeed caused some trials to be halted due to judicial misconduct.

Edward Peters (2002, pp. 238-241) demonstrates that, while the *Malleus* has come down in the popular imagination as exemplifying mainstream late medieval misogyny, in fact Kramer's attitudes were highly atypical, and his colleagues, even within the Inquisition, found him an embarrassment. His book, however, was not aimed at fellow inquisitors but at (equally skeptical) lay magistrates, as an attempt to make them understand the terrible threat that witches held for Christian society. In some cases, his arguments actually backfired, causing some judges who might have been inclined to believe in witchcraft to dismiss the entire topic due to Kramer's excesses. Others, however, swallowed it hook, line, and sinker.

One of the chief arenas for the spread of these new ideas about witchcraft was at Church councils, such as those at Constance in 1414-1418 and Basel in 1431-1439. These informational clearing-houses brought together clerics and laymen from throughout Europe and sent them home with new suspicions about evil in their midst. The spread of belief in diabolical witchcraft in the fifteenth century follows much the same pattern as belief in Satanic ritual abuse in the 1980s and 1990s; in Britain, for instance, the massive Satanic ritual abuse scares at Cleveland, Rochedale, and the Orkneys directly followed social workers attending workshops on the topic organized by fundamentalist American groups. Once the idea of secretive obscenities is planted in the minds of those charged with combating such threats, the evil is seen everywhere, whether it exists or not.

Once the stereotype of the witch was established in the minds of those who were in a position to prosecute such crimes, the next necessary step for the witch hunts was to find some witches. This was greatly facilitated by the increasing acceptance of torture as a method of questioning the accused. Early European law, especially in Celtic and Germanic areas (where the witch hunts were most virulent), was based on maintaining social balance through local courts (a "jury of one's peers") and a system of fines for various crimes, based on the status of the victim, literally his "face value." Law kicked in after a crime was committed, and its intent was to make things even through financial recompense. As European society became more centralized, with fewer and more powerful rulers, the judicial system also became more centralized, with judges sent from, or at least accountable to, a distant potentate. As Bengt Ankarloo points out (2002, p. 64), while this meant that intimacy and familiarity with local conditions was lost, it also meant that law was less likely to be used as a tool for working out small-town hostilities. What centralized government and centralized law did provide was the notion that law should prevent crime before it occurred through the threat of horrible punishments. Witchcraft was viewed as an exceptional crime that required exceptional means—like torture—to stamp it out.

The use of torture to extract confessions, whether of witchcraft or other malfeasance, was always viewed with suspicion, since it was readily recognized that people would confess to just about anything to make the torture stop, if it were severe enough. Nonetheless, once in the grip of a conviction that the Devil was afoot, otherwise reasonable people would lose their rational qualms about the reliability of confessions obtained through torture and keep going as long as there was information to be extracted.

The tortures they inflicted were truly obscene and often showed an obsession with probing women's bodies in a nearly pornographic manner. They were stripped and every square inch of their bodies stuck with a pin to find the "witches' mark" that was impervious to pain. Of course, every part that was not a witches' mark did feel the pain. They were placed on the rack, with their limbs pulled in opposite directions until the joints broke. The strappado also broke bones and joints by pulling the victim up to the ceiling by their hands, bound behind their back, and then abruptly dropped so that the entire weight of the body jerked their arms from their sockets. Their fingernails were torn off with pincers and needles inserted in their nail beds. Metal boots were placed around their legs that crushed their bones and flesh to a pulp; the thumbscrews did the same to fingers. A clawlike device called the spider was heated and used to tear off pieces of flesh; in some cases, women's breasts were torn off their bodies. Heated irons were thrust in all available orifices, boiling water poured down throats. In addition to the test of throwing suspected witches into a stream or pond with their hands tied to their feet, to see whether the pure water rejected the impure witch (in which case they floated) or accepted them (in which case they sunk), suspected witches were also tested by having their limbs thrust into boiling water. Scalds—the natural result of boiling water on flesh—indicated guilt (Bartel 2000, pp. 63-64).

What the tortures really show, however, is that whether they were inflicted on female or male bodies, the torturers had reached the point where they had ceased to regard their victims as human, possibly not even as animal. Witches were said to leave their bodies in order to travel to the witches' sabbath in spirit; the tortures inflicted on accused witches worked to disintegrate and deconstruct those bodies, transgressing the integrity of their natural boundaries by crushing and tearing the flesh. If witches operated on the spiritual plane, then destroying their bodies left them nothing to return to, no means of spreading their evil through the human world. Except, of course, that these people were not witches; even if they were folk healers or even malicious cursers of their neighbors, the evidence for organized worship of Satan, even without his corporeal appearance to bestow favors, is virtually nonexistent.

One of the most frustrating aspects of understanding the witch hunts is that no one explanation covers all the bases, and many explanations seem equally to account for many events. This suggests that calling them witch "crazes" really is the most suitable terminology; these are events that are overdetermined, in Sigmund Freud's sense of mental events (such as dreams) that have many underlying causes and inspirations, resulting in a single image, narrative, or event. Some of these underlying causes might be physical—as in the theory that people's beliefs that they flew to orgiastic sabbaths were caused by ergot poisoning, or the psychoactive ingredients in the flying ointment—or they might be the result of social tensions—extrapolating the "demonization" of the Catholic or Protestant religions to create the idea of a literally demonic religion—or they might be psychological—projecting male, especially priestly or monkish (and therefore celibate) anxiety about sexuality onto women, or even turning thwarted sexual urges into hatred for women, which is expressed through torturing female bodies.

Mary Beth Norton recently suggested that the Salem witch craze of 1692 was caused by sublimated anxieties about the atrocities committed by Native Americans during King William's War (Norton 2002). She points out that many of the people who were involved in the Salem witch trials had recently come to the Salem area from Maine, refugees from Indian massacres. The accusations made against "witches" track very closely with actual mutilations that occurred in these massacres. This is one case where the process of projection can be very clearly demonstrated, although, again, it does not provide a complete explanation for why there, why then.

Similarly, William Monter compares the occurrences of witch manias in the realms of the Catholic brothers Maximilian and Ferdinand of Bavaria (Monter 2002, pp. 22-31). Maximilian put a firm halt to witch trials in his domain, while Ferdinand presided over one of the most virulent hunts in history. Monter comes to the conclusion that, in general terms, witch hunts took place in small or midsize jurisdictions with little central governmental control. Contrary to most modern assumptions, it was local, secular courts that had the highest rates of torture and execution of witches, not the centralized, clerical courts such as the Inquisition. Without outside eyes to assess any underlying tensions that could be causing accusations, a kind of mass hysteria did indeed arise that caught large numbers of people in its grip, as both victims and perpetrators. Often, what brought a witch mania to an end was the accusation of a person who was so self-evidently *not* a witch that the accusation slapped some sense into those who had been carried along on the tide of terror. By this time, it was usually too late for many other equally innocent people.

The analyses of Monter, Angkarloo, Clark, and many other scholars suggest, however, that perhaps the most influential factor in the course of witch crazes throughout the medieval and early modern eras was specific individuals. This was an age when a single person, such as Heinrich Kramer or Matthew Hopkins, the notorious "Witchfinder General" of the Cromwellian era in Britain, could have an enormous impact by the mere strength of their conviction and force of their personality. The right—or wrong—combination of personalities, bad weather, germs, a bitter love affair, an abusive parent, a book falling into someone's hands or a lecture heard at a church council, a story told by an effective narrator on a moonless night, or a nightmare, could spark the judicial murder of half a village. The presence of one immovable skeptic could stop it. Certain technicalities, such as the admission of torture as a tool for extracting confessions, could fan the flames into a wildfire. Contrary to modern American political values, which tend to view strong centralized government as potentially despotic and which promote the superiority of local knowledge, it would appear that the rulers who had the most absolutist tendencies in the early modern era were the ones most able to quell witch crazes within their realms.

Modern Wiccans point out, rightly, that they cannot be Satanists because Satan is a an aspect of Christianity and they are not Christians. A similar argument could be made for the magical practitioners of the medieval and early modern worlds—although these magicians, cunning folk, healers, and diviners belonged to the Christian church, they regarded their magic as belonging to a different aspect of life from religion. They called upon God, Jesus, Mary, and especially the angels to give power to their spells and charms, and they drew on the mystique attached to books and literacy—things introduced by and under the control of Christianity—to give themselves the aura of power and status. From their point of view, the entire spectrum of the supernatural was the creation, and under the domain, of God.

The Church's point of view was equally simple, but rather more dichotomous: the Church had purview over the good supernatural, and anything supernatural that was not part of its organization was, by definition, demonic. This view was a reaction to the tumultuous times of the fourteenth through seventeenth centuries—an age of plague, war, famine, massive social disruption, and especially religious controversy. The Reformation was sparked by a growing belief that the Church had gone lax, perhaps even provoking the disasters afflicting society as punishment for its laxity (the Old Testament offered ample testimony to God's predilection for smiting his people when they strayed from the straight and narrow); the Counter-Reformation attempted to clean Catholicism's spiritual house so that the Protestants' accusations would no longer hold water. From both directions, therefore, anything that smacked of illicit spirituality could only arise from the Devil. Shades of gray were no longer tolerated.

Both Catholics and Protestants collapsed all the variations of magical belief and practice into one category, which they defined: the diabolic. First they created a hysterical, conspiratorial vision of the forces that opposed the Church, and then they forced the entire magical world to conform to that vision. Carlo Ginzburg's research on the *benandanti* shows how the Inquisition slowly, over the course of a century or more, twisted the popular conception of these shamanic spiritual travelers, even among the *benandanti* themselves, from being the force that battled witches to being witches themselves. For the next three centuries, there would be only one kind of magic.

CHAPTER 6

WEIRD SISTERS AND NOBLE WIZARDS

THE PEAK OF THE EUROPEAN WITCH HUNTS occurred between 1560 and 1660. For an era of both rapid social change and heightened artistic output, it would be almost impossible to cover the entire spectrum of European literature and popular culture for its representations of witches, witchcraft, and magic. At the risk of succumbing to Anglophone bias, however, the plays of William Shakespeare fall comfortably right in the middle of this period—his career as an actor and playwright in London lasted from around 1592 to 1613—and contain some of the most well-known representations of Renaissance magic.

Furthermore, Shakespeare's influence has been felt far beyond the boundaries of English literature, and the spin Shakespeare put on nearly all of his topics, from British history to tragedy, has become the Western cultural norm: Richard III was an evil hunchback, Romeo and Juliet are the archetype of romantic love, and things would have been a lot better for everyone if Macbeth hadn't listened to those witches.

Witchcraft was an important topic during Shakespeare's life. Elizabeth's statute against witchcraft was enacted in 1563, the year before his birth. Reginald Scot's skeptical analysis, *The Discoverie of Witchcraft*, was published in 1584, while King James's *Demonologie*, a work that actively promoted the belief in maleficent magic, appeared in 1597 and, in 1604, James, now king of England as well as of Scotland, enacted his own witchcraft statute. Ten major witchcraft trials took place in England between 1566 and 1612. During this period, there was a major shift from a general disinclination among those in authority to take witchcraft as a realistic and serious offense to a willingness to believe in witchcraft and to execute people for practicing it.

In England's first witchcraft statute, enacted under Henry VIII in 1542, a spectrum of activities was defined as felonious, including conjuring spirits, using magic to find treasure or to cause another person bodily harm or loss of goods, to manipulate love, to discover the whereabouts of stolen goods, or for any other unlawful end. Although this pretty much covers all the traditional uses of magic, the purpose of the statute seems very much to be the punishment of antisocial magical activities, and guilt depended upon the magician or witch's intent. The 1563 statute, enacted by Henry's daughter Elizabeth after a tumultuous period of religious upheaval. During this period, Protestants and Catholics, alternately in power, each took advantage of their situation to persecute the other. Elizabeth's statute again defined maleficent magic in terms of its intent and its impact on society, and although it was more inclined to define the very desire to practice *maleficium* as injurious to the community, it was somewhat more lenient in its punishments: witchcraft only became a capital crime on the second offense.

It was James's statute of 1604 that made it a crime to commune with evil spirits in any way and for any purpose, a change in which Keith Thomas sees the influence of Continental theories of the diabolical nature of witchcraft yet which still left a loophole for those magicians who claimed to communicate with good spirits (Thomas 1971, pp. 442-443).

Within this cultural milieu, it is perhaps surprising that there are not more witches in Shakespeare. However, magic and the supernatural are woven throughout the plays in a number of ways and in a variety of contexts. In *Hamlet* (1601) there is, for instance, the ghost of Hamlet's father, an entity that sets in motion the entire action of the play. Although he only appears at the very beginning, the very notion of the ghost lays out one of the major themes of the play: what do you trust? From a skeptical, rationalist point of view, a ghost is a mere illusion and anything that a ghost might say would be of no value. In fact, one might view a person who sees ghosts as somewhat mad. The ghost communicates only with Hamlet, whose subsequent behavior seems mad to those who aren't privy to his mental processes, and the ghost's communication concretizes the vague misgivings that have been lurking in the back of Hamlet's mind. So, when Hamlet "acts" insane, which is the result of his communicating with a ghost, his behavior merely confirms the views of those who thought that he really was insane all along. Yet from the point of view of the audience, which sees Hamlet's interaction with his father's ghost, the ghost is real and his information is correct, and Hamlet's subsequent actions are completely rational—even though their end result is to wipe out the entire royal family and most of the court, as well as to cause one case of legitimate insanity.

From either point of view, the intervention of the supernatural in the natural world has a tragic outcome and, more particularly, overthrows the political realm disastrously. Remember that magic was frequently used as a means to political ends in medieval courts, whether as an active means to influence political fortunes and favors or as a useful accusation to discredit one's political opponents. Magic was a way of using the supernatural to affect one's political situation. In *Hamlet*, the appearance of the ghost is at once both a literal and metaphorical representation of this tactic. As a "real" ghost, he is the supernatural personified; as a "fake" ghost, he symbolizes the dangers of calling the supernatural into the natural world.

Horatio dismisses the ghost as a fantasy until he sees it with his own eyes, but once convinced of its reality, he is immediately assailed with (prescient) political forebodings. He recalls the omens that attended the assassination of Julius Caesar (omens Shakespeare had incorporated in his own play on the subject two years previously). Hamlet, upon seeing his father's ghost, leaves it open whether it may come from heaven or hell, whether it is a "spirit of health or goblin damned," even whether it is, in fact, his father or a demon taking his father's form. The ghost ultimately reveals that he was poisoned by his brother to steal both his throne and his wife—an act that he explicitly describes as witchcraft (*Hamlet* I, v). The supernatural in *Hamlet* falls firmly within the arena of medieval and early modern political "magic," and by breaking the normal boundaries between life and death, natural and supernatural, initiates a cascade of boundary-breaking that ultimately grinds all of Denmark's government into a chaos that can only be restored by bringing in a ruler who has had no stake in this disintegration—Fortinbras.

Four years or so previously, Shakespeare had already presented a picture of political wizardry in a most literal sense in *I Henry IV* (1597). Here the figure of Owen Glendower appears as a mad Welshman in a stereotype that can be traced back to Taliesin, Merlin, and all the other mad poet/warriors of the Middle Ages. Shakespeare makes a deliberate contrast between Glendower's operatic claims to "call spirits from the vasty deep" and Hotspur's skeptical retort, "But will they come when you do call them?" (*I Henry IV* III, i). Glendower claims privileged status because the earth trembled when he was born; Hotspur charges that this is hubris, to assume that, of all the things that might have happened on that day and at that time, it was Glendower's birth specifically that this omen foretold. The entire scene contrasts the sane, skeptical Englishman and the wild, poetic Welshman, the one embodying the scientific mindset of the Renaissance while the other exemplifies the medieval worldview of backwards Wales.

Glendower, however, has a foot in both worlds: he was schooled at court in London and can speak English, unlike his daughter, who cannot even communicate with her English husband, Mortimer, except through gesture, song, and her father's translation. The leitmotif of the scene is the unintelligibility of the Welsh language; even when he is speaking English, Glendower's most metaphorical and poetic outbursts are labeled by the others as "Welsh" and therefore incomprehensible. Hotspur complains that the previous evening, Glendower had kept him up for nine hours enumerating the "several devil's names/That were his lackeys," and yet, once Lady Mortimer sings in her native language, he exclaims that "the Devil understands Welsh" and that this reveals that "he is a good musician"—although Hotspur himself would rather listen to his dog howl in Irish (ibid.)

Owein Glyndŵr (to give him his Welsh spelling) was born around 1354 and, after a life spent very much in the sphere of the English court and military, rose in rebellion against Henry IV in 1400; although there were many personal reasons for the break between the Welsh nobleman and the English king, many of Glyndŵr's countrymen joined him in outrage over excessive taxation. Glyndŵr acquired a magical reputation through his unexpected victories against the English but even more through the uncanny coincidences of bad weather that dogged the English army every time they tried to invade Wales. Controlling the weather is, of course, one of the classic skills of the witch. Glyndŵr's reputation was cemented when, rather than falling in battle or submitting to the Crown when the tide finally turned around 1415, he simply disappeared. Modern scholars suspect that he simply took refuge with his daughter and her family in Herefordshire and lived out his life in obscurity.

Glyndŵr also made the transition to Welsh folk hero, becoming a hero of a type known as the "sleeping redeemer," the savior of the Welsh who slumbers in a cave, waiting for the hour of Wales' greatest need, when he will awake and drive the enemy from the land once and for all. King Arthur is probably the most well-known example of this type, and Frederick Barbarossa in Germany, Charlemagne in France, Holger Danske in Denmark, and Prince Marko in Serbia are also said to wait for their hours. Unlike the English, Germans, French, Danes, or Serbs, however, the Welsh have redeemers sleeping under every third rock: not only Arthur and Owein Glyndŵr, but also Hiriell, Cadwaladr, Cynan Meriadoc, an unspecified Owein (a popular name and a popular name for redeemers), and Owein Lawgoch.

Elissa Henken, in her perceptive study *National Redeemer: Owain Glyndŵr in Welsh Tradition* (1996), points out that Glyndŵr has a multifaceted character in Welsh folklore: trickster, master of escape, social outlaw, culture hero, native nobleman and warrior, destroyer, avenger, magician, and folk hero in local, national, and international contexts. She notes that the perception of him as a magician because of his alleged command of the weather was very much an English one;

"The Welsh, on the other hand, perhaps knowing the peculiarities of their weather too well to ascribe to it any supernatural explanation, note the same events with, at the most, some disparagement for the outsider unable to cope with the Welsh terrain and weather, and some pride in Glyndŵr's skill in the use of guerilla tactics" (Henken 1996, p. 134). Magic, it would seem, is indeed very much in the eye of the beholder.

Shakespeare's depiction of the "wizard" Glendower clings to this interpretation: Glendower is a magician because he is incomprehensible and Welsh. He talks a good talk, but ultimately, his mysterious power is simply his mysterious words, and otherwise he is simply a clever warrior who can grab the advantages that come his way. Although Shakespeare does not advance this point, it seems significant that in his scene of Hotspur, Mortimer, and Glendower making plans to overthrow the king and divide Britain between themselves, Glendower is the one with the most legitimate claim to a separate country, at least from the Welsh point of view. Magic, once again, is the tool of politics, a means of conjuring a kingdom where none existed before.

The magical world of *A Midsummer Night's Dream* is in stark contrast to the political magic of the tragedy of *Hamlet* and the history of *I Henry IV*. The fact that this play is a comedy is certainly relevant; however, even in the realm of love and marriage, the political realm is not completely absent. Parallel to both the proposed human marriages of Theseus and Hippolyta, on the one hand, and Hermia, Helena, Demetrius, and Lysander (in varying combinations) in the other is the fraught fairy marriage between Oberon and Titania. The two sets of noble lovers, human and fairy, sandwich the two sets of non-noble lovers. The marriages of Hermia, Helena, Demetrius, and Lysander are of importance chiefly for the emotional happiness of the pairs and secondarily (in that Hermia does not wish to marry her father's choice of spouse) in upholding the laws and customs of human society; the marriages between Theseus and Hippolyta, Oberon and Titania, have repercussions beyond their personal pleasures. Theseus's betrothal is a consequence of his military victory over the Amazons—a female society that itself subverts and inverts "normal" patriarchal society. Hippolyta's marriage to Theseus will therefore indicate female submission to the male in a very vital sense. Oberon and Titania, as fairies, invert and subvert the human realm: they are small where humans are large, their activities take place largely at night rather than during the day, they live in the forest where humans live in cities and towns, they perform magic where humans have magic performed upon them, and interestingly enough, in terms of gender roles, Oberon has had a long interest in Hippolyta's career while Titania has assisted Theseus in his various amours.

Shakespeare sets out the characteristics of his fairies in their first scene. Puck, or Robin Goodfellow, is a hobgoblin type of fairy, and his main task is to sew discord and screw things up. He frightens the village girls, leads travelers astray, prevents the butter from coming in the churn and the beer from fermenting, and is responsible for all the messy accidents of daily life, like missing the chair when you try to sit down or the beer you're drinking spilling all over your shirt. Nonetheless, for those who respect him and treat him well, he will do their chores and make the household run smoothly. Notice, however, that many of these talents, especially magicking the butter and the beer, are traditional maleficent acts of witches. Furthermore, the boy who is the source of Oberon and Titania's quarrel is a changeling, a boy stolen by the fairies and a sickly fairy child left in his place. When Titania refuses to yield the child to Oberon, the king of the fairies decides to use the juice of a magical plant to enchant Titania into falling in love with an ugly animal so that he may blackmail her into giving up the changeling boy. Here, again, we see the use of magic as a means of inducing inappropriate sexual desire.

Naturally the love-juice goes astray and wackiness ensues. Oberon luckily has another juice that reverses his spells and sets to with it when he has acquired his changeling boy from his deluded wife. The judicious application of potions to this one and that one guarantees that each lover winds up happy with his or her partner, and even Titania does not appear to regret her magically induced surrender of the changeling. Yet despite the happy ending, the question remains open as to how sinister the fairy folk may be. Puck warns Oberon that the magic must be settled quickly because morning approaches, when

> ghosts, wand'ring here and there,
> Troop home to churchyards; damned spirits all,

That in crossways and floods have burial,
Already to their wormy beds are gone
For fear lest day should look their shames upon,
They willfully themselves exile from light,
And must for aye consort with black-browed night.
(*Midsummer Night's Dream* III, ii).

Oberon protests that he is perfectly capable of operating in daytime and "with the Morning's love hath oft made sport" (ibid.), but nonetheless, it would be better to get the whole situation wound up before dawn. Puck returns to the theme of the fairies' association with night and death in the final scene, when he comes in literally to sweep up after the happy resolution of the lovers' plights:

Now the hungry lion roars,
And the wolf bemoans the moon;
Whilst the heavy ploughman snores,
All with weary task foredone.
Now the wasted brands do glow,
Whilst the screech owl, screeching loud,
Puts the wretch that lies in woe
In remembrance of a shroud.
Now it is the time of night
That the graves, all gaping wide,
Every one lets forth his sprite,
In the churchway paths to glide.
And we fairies, that do run
By the triple Hecate's team
From the presence of the sun,
Following darkness like a dream,
Now are frolic.
(*Midsummer Night's Dream* V, i)

Puck makes clear the connection between fairies and Hecate, the goddess of witches, the goddess worshiped by Medea and all her classical kin. It seems appropriate that it is Puck, the trickster fairy, who undercuts his master's claims of sweetness and light, first by causing the romantic mix-ups that affect the young lovers and then by consistently reminding Oberon and the audience of the fairy folk's darker allegiances.

The fairies of *A Midsummer Night's Dream* remind us of the ambiguous line between witches and fairies that persisted throughout the Middle Ages. Both perform magic, but fairies did so by their innate magic while witches had to sell their souls to the Devil or else force, persuade, or trick the real magical beings—fairies, demons, daimons, what have you—to do it for them. In this sense, it is possible to see Oberon as a witch, committing magic by means of his "familiar" Puck. Oberon himself does not make magic, but uses his observation of the natural (and unnatural) world to take advantage of the universe's innate magic—in this case, noticing where Cupid's arrow went astray and infected a plant with its love-inducing properties—and then commands his supernatural underlings to make the magic themselves.

Early modern demonologists constructed a fantasy of a demonic witchy gathering that inverted the human gathering of the church; the fairy world here is another type of inversion of human society. The actions of the fairies contain the same threats to human society that witchcraft does; even though romantic mishaps are the stuff of comedy, taken too far, they do venture into the territory of universal infertility that is the underlying threat of witchcraft. Hermia's options are to marry a man she loathes, to become a celibate, or to be executed. The latter two options are merely two different forms of physical infertility, while the first dooms her to a life of emotional infertility. Titiania's love for Bottom, who has been turned into an ass, crosses two different kind of species lines—fairy/human and human/animal. It also recalls Apuleius's tenure as an ass, and the threat that he might have to engage in sexual intercourse with a murderess. It is interesting that Titania is in many respects the fairy version of Hippolyta, a woman whose name means "stampeding horse," and the product of the union of a horse and an ass is a mule, an animal that is sterile. Oberon creates a sterile love in his wife in order to spirit a child from her, a child who is already a changeling, now doubly so. This double-negative then creates the circumstances to allow the (fertile) union of the other three couples.

A Midsummer Night's Dream is one of the Shakespeare's earlier plays (c. 1595); the twists and turns and disruptions of magic leading to fruitful union is also a theme of one of his last, *The Tempest* (1611). Yet the political facet of magic is also visible in this play. The magician Prospero is the deposed duke of Milan; ironically, his brother Antonio usurped his dukedom while Prospero's attention was distracted with his (magical) studies. Prospero and his then-infant daughter Miranda were set adrift, with nothing but a little food and Prospero's most precious books, and propitiously landed on an enchanted island. Here the magician commands a host of spirits, especially Ariel, and the monster Caliban: Caliban is the son of the witch Sycorax; Ariel is a spirit who had been Sycorax's servant, imprisoned by her in a cloven pine and released by Prospero to be his slave. Just as Prospero believes that his brother unjustly usurped his dukedom, thinking that because he did all the work of the duke he should be the duke, Caliban believes that Prospero has usurped his rule of the island, after first pretending to be his friend and caring for him until Caliban had revealed all the secrets of the island.

Ariel is described as an "airy sprite;" in fact, he is the Renaissance version of a daimon. Prospero commands Ariel in the manner of a classical Renaissance magician. One of the inspirations for Prospero may have Dr. John Dee, a true Renaissance man whose researches led him from astrology and alchemy, mathematics, cryptography, architecture, and the Kabbalah to communication with angels—airy spirits—through his friend Edward Kelley by scrying in a crystal ball or other reflective surface. Dee and Kelley claimed to have received dictation from these spirits in a cryptic alphabet they called Enochian, after the biblical patriarch Enoch who "walked with God." Dee was considered one of the leading Hermetic, Rosicrucian thinkers of his time, a school of occult wisdom whose roots trailed back to the classical Neoplatonism of Plotinus and his followers.

In passing, it should be noted that Dee, although born and raised in England and a graduate of Cambridge University, was the son of a Welshman, making him in many ways analogous to Shakespeare's other Anglo-Welsh wizard, Owen Glendower. "Dee" is an anglicization of Welsh *du*, "black" or "swarthy," a common nickname in an era when the Welsh did not have surnames per se, but also an appropriate name for one who studied what would come to be known as the "black arts." Dee was popularly credited with having summoned the storm that sunk the Spanish Armada before it could invade England; Glyndŵr was believed to have thwarted the English army's attempts to quell his uprising in Wales by raising storms, while Glendower claims to have sent the English "bootless home and weather-beaten back;" Prospero raises the tempest of the play's title in order to shipwreck his brother and wreak his revenge.

Propero's magic is of a more studious nature than that of Glendower and of a more human nature than that of the fairies of *A Midsummer Night's Dream*. His magic is something he has acquired through study in books, just as one might study history or physics. Glendower's magic appears to come from oral tradition and his power, as far as he believes, is innate in him, as announced by the portents that attended his birth. The magic of the fairies is likewise innate in their race; they fly just as birds fly, because they're built that way. Magic is something that makes fairies, and even the Welsh, "Other." Prospero is no different from any other human, except that he has made a study of the ways in which to control elements of nature that most other people consider to be beyond their power. The sprites and spirits whom Prospero commands are not demons or devils, but anthropomorphicized nature.

Prospero's magic is contrasted with that of the witch Sycorax. Although her deeds are not enumerated beyond her confining Ariel in a tree trunk, they were dreadful enough to warrant her execution. However, she was merely exiled to the island—like those accused of witchcraft in early modern Europe, the fact that she was pregnant required a stay of her punishment. Sycorax's power derived from her worship of a "god" called Setebos, who is presumably the "Devil" who begot Caliban upon her. Sycorax and her son Caliban are the inversion of Prospero and his daughter Miranda: female, demonic magic that produces monsters versus male, literate magic that produces beauty. (Many critics have discussed the further dimension that Sycrorax, a North African from Angiers, and Caliban, putatively West Indian, contrast with the European Prospero and Miranda as a calque on Renaissance imperialism.) However, Prospero is perfectly capable of imprisoning Ariel in a tree trunk just as Sycorax had done, and threatens to do so if Ariel doesn't carry out his orders willingly and without question. Sycorax's ugliness is repeatedly referred to, reflecting the contemporary belief that appearance really does represent an individual's personal and moral value. Sycorax is ugly, therefore she is evil, or she is evil and therefore ugly; cause and effect are not particularly relevant. Similarly, Prospero wears a special robe when he performs his magic. By putting on the uniform, and thus the appearance, of a magician, he becomes a magician. This correspondence between external appearance and internal reality provides a bedrock underneath the illusions and delusions that superficially confuse the inhabitants—permanent or temporary—of the island.

The contrast between Prospero and Sycorax and their magics reflects a dichotomy in the classification of magic that arose in the early Christian era but became particularly important in the early modern period. On the one hand is the traditional, orally transmitted magic generally practiced by women and/or the lower classes and the elite, erudite magic practiced by intellectual, literate males. Both types of magic had overlapping interests—divination, the discovery of treasure, and recovery of stolen goods—but were increasingly in conflict as the secularizing tendency of Renaissance scholarship began to divorce the study of healing and of the forces of nature from religion. Magic evolved into science and medicine at the elite level, and in the process of realizing that many of the "mysteries" of the natural world were comprehensible, the magical understanding of the world fell into disrepute.

In the Middle Ages, although the Church did not smile upon magic, it was possible to see miraculous or magical events as deriving from good religion when performed by clerics and saints or bad religion when performed by others, especially pagans. The Renaissance removed religion from the equation, and just as Protestants and Catholics both were inclined to dismiss other religions as mere superstitions, so early scientists were inclined to dismiss folk medicine and folk magic as delusions and superstitions. At the same time, the two strands of early modern magic can still be seen in operation in the modern era as ceremonial magic and Neopaganism.

One of the major themes of *The Tempest* is right political succession. Antonio, who stole Prospero's dukedom, takes advantage of

Ferdinand's apparent death in the tempest to propose to Sebastian, Alonso's brother, that now is a propitious time to usurp the kingship of Naples. Parallel to this conspiracy is Caliban's plan, formulated with the jester Trinculo and the drunken butler Stephano, to overthrow Prospero and take the rule of the island to themselves. Ferdinand is overwrought at Alonso's apparent death and regards his seeming ascension to the throne as an occasion of grief since it can only occur as a result of his parent's death, and his willingness to labor as Prospero's prisoner indicates a virtuous disregard for status and power in favor of love for Miranda. Prospero has engineered the entire situation in order to regain his dukedom, even though he seems to have little interest in rule per se; rather, the displacement of the rightful ruler, no matter how unworldly, overthrows the proper hierarchy of society and thus threatens the proper order of the world.

This play very much advances a belief in the divine right of kings—it is more important to be born a ruler than to be temperamentally suited for being one. When human machinations have usurped the "natural" social order, magic is required to restore it. Yet Prospero also renounces his magic when it is time to return to his dukedom. Political power or magical power—you can have one or the other, but not both.

Shakespeare's most notorious witches appear in *Macbeth* (c. 1605). Once again, magic has disruptive effects on the political sphere. Would Macbeth have become king even if he had not encountered the witches? If he were truly destined to be king, might his kingship have had a happier ending if he had come by it legitimately? Was the entire tale in all its particulars fated from the beginning? Or did the witches create the whole situation out of their innate wickedness and a fiendish desire to disrupt the social order?

In case the audience is wondering who these three women are who have appeared on stage, their first exchange concerns the raising of a storm in order to torment the sailor-husband of a woman who offended one of them by not sharing her chestnuts. Well then, they must be witches, because that's what witches do: storms, malice, begging, body parts, some details eternal to European witchcraft and some specific to the Tudor and Stuart era. However, they call themselves the "weird" sisters, a word that derives from the Norse and Old English concept of "wyrd" or fate, and thus harken back to the notion of three sister-goddesses who sit at the base of the world tree and determine the destiny of every human. Their elliptical references to the destinies of both Macbeth and Banquo fall into this tradition, and also link to the Celtic belief in a goddess of sovereignty who must confirm each king.

An Irish legend about the origin of the Uí Néill, who claimed the "high kingship of Tara" for most of the early Middle Ages, traced the family back to Niall Noígiallach (Niall of the Nine Hostages) who was the son of King Eochu Mugmedón by a slave woman named Cairenn. How did the son of a slave become a king? One day Niall and his four brothers—legitimate sons of the king—were out hunting and got lost. They stopped for the night and decided to cook some of the meat they had killed during the day, but they had no water to boil it. Each brother in turn wandered into the woods and encountered an ugly hag who offered them water in exchange for a kiss. Three of the brothers refused outright; Fiachra barely brushed her cheek with his lips, while Niall not only kissed her but had sex with her as well. When he did so, the hag turned into a supernaturally beautiful young woman who announced that she was the Sovereignty of Ireland and that Niall's descendants would be kings of Ireland from then on, except for two kings who would be of Fiachra's line (Mac Cana 1983, pp. 119-120).

Although Niall lived over half a millennium earlier than Macbeth and even the hegemony of the Uí Néill, across the Irish Sea, was waning in the eleventh century, the similarities between Niall's encounter in the woods with a supernatural woman who predicts his kingship as well as the kingship of descendants of one of his companions, and Macbeth's encounter with three supernatural women who predict the same for him and his companion, suggest that this is a Celtic mythological motif that worked its way into the history compiled by Raphael Holinshed that was Shakespeare's source.

Nick Aitchison has thoroughly traced the evolution from the historical Macbeth—a king who appears to have been quite well regarded by his peers, or at least by the poets he paid to praise himself—to Shakespeare's villain (Aitchison 1999). As with so much medieval mythology, political agendas provide the spin that outlasts the hero's death. John of Fordun, in the 1360s, was the first chronicler to recount essentially the story as related by Shakespeare, in which Macbeth is an assassin, usurper, and tyrant.

However, it was Andrew of Wyntoun who, in his *Orygynale Cronykil of Scotland* written in the 1410s, truly demonized the king: Andrew relates that Macbeth's mother, walking alone in the woods, encountered a handsome stranger with whom she had sex and thereby conceived Macbeth by the Devil himself. This story seems, superficially, to have some connection with the idea of witches' sabbaths held in the wilderness, where witches have sex with the Devil, but in fact, since it takes place in the daytime and the woman is alone, it really bears more resemblance to Celtic myths in which a hero is conceived when his mother, walking in a liminal, uninhabited area such as a forest or the seashore, meets a handsome fairy. It is in this way that the Irish mythological king Brés is conceived—a king who, incidentally, becomes a great tyrant.

Andrew of Wyntoun also introduces the "weird sisters" who predict Macbeth's future greatness, although he sees them in a dream as a teenager rather than in the flesh as an adult. The prophecy that Macbeth can only be slain by a "man not born of a woman" is announced by his devilish father immediately after his conception. As Aitchison points out, "As the Devil's son, Macbeth can only be killed by someone of 'unnatural' birth" (Aitchison 1999, p. 111). Aitchison also notes that the main events of Macbeth's life as recounted by Andrew of Wyntoun fall into the standard genres of what Proinsias Mac Cana has termed the "learned tales of medieval Ireland" (Mac Cana 1980): conceptions and births, dreams and visions, invasions, battles, and violent deaths. Thus, although Andrew's *Chronykil* is decidedly hostile to Macbeth, it also turns a historical personage into a figure of mainstream Celtic myth. However, this happens precisely at the time that the mythological and supernatural beliefs of northern Europe are becoming redemonized by the Church. The Otherworldly sire turns from a fairy to the Devil, the prophesying women—druidesses?—into witches.

Hector Boece's *Scotorum Historiae*, published in 1527, cranked up the supernatural element in Macbeth's history another notch or two. He was the first to name the "weird sisters" as witches and also introduced the character of Banquo—a fictional figure who provided a duly prophesied origin for the Stewarts, the family of the then king, James V. From the very first, Banquo made a postmortem appearance as a ghost. In contrast to earlier chroniclers who had represented the witches' prophecy as a statement of fact, if one with several catches, Boece also introduced the elaboration that the prophecy itself planted the seed in Macbeth's mind to make it real through murder and usurpation, egged on by his ambitious wife.

As with *Hamlet*, *I Henry IV*, and *The Tempest*, magic in *Macbeth* signifies the disruption of the social and political hierarchy. Whether through controlling the weather or controlling a weak man's mind, the supernatural intervenes to disrupt and corrupt the natural. This is perhaps one of the hardest things to appreciate for a Western, twenty-first century mind that takes for granted the popular conception of the second law of thermodynamics: everything tends toward chaos. Or, as William Butler Yeats put it so succinctly, "Things fall apart." We assume that disorder and movement are the natural state of the universe; any semblance of order and organization is achieved only with the expenditure of great amounts of energy and only maintained with even more energy.

There are both positive and negative sides to this belief. The negative is that order is almost more trouble than it is worth. The positive is that the dissolution of order also creates the circumstances for change and, by extension, freedom. In a society that is premised on the belief that people can make anything of themselves that they may wish, provided they work hard enough, an organized and ordered universe in which everything has a place and must stay there is one definition of, if not hell, at least prison.

The medieval and early modern world had a very different view of the operation of the universe. God had created a perfect world in perfect order. All you had to do to exist in God's perfect world was stay put and don't rock the boat. The fact that things did go wrong, that things fell apart, was a sign that the Devil was at work, doing his best to corrupt God's perfection with imperfection. Human acts that disrupted God's natural order—whether attempting to divine the future, begging for food from your neighbors because you had no one to support you, producing a more abundant harvest than your neighbors even though your fields didn't seem any different than theirs, or making so much money in your business that you could move out of the hovel you were born in and into a mansion—aroused suspicions that the Devil was at work.

Even natural events, such as storms, earthquakes, and eclipses, made it uncomfortably clear that the usual organization of the world was falling apart, and therefore there might very well be devilishly inspired humans somewhere working to create this chaos. The increase in social—and geographical—mobility in the early modern era was both liberating and threatening, and the possible dangers posed by change were very much on the contemporary mind. These dangers were easily projected onto the figure of the witch. Likewise, political misdeeds that disrupt the natural order, such as the assassinations committed by Macbeth in Scotland and by Claudius in Denmark, are revealed by ghosts, messengers from the supernatural world.

Although at one level the skepticism of the early modern age was a precursor of the modern scientific worldview that dismissed magic and witchcraft as delusions because such things simply couldn't happen, Renaissance skepticism grew out of a medieval worldview that such things didn't happen because God had decreed otherwise. The modern worldview, in contrast, holds that such things can't happen because the laws of nature decree otherwise. The medieval and early modern, religiously based approach did still allow for the uncanny and the unnatural, however, on the understanding that it was God's prerogative to allow the occasional exemption from the norm, generally to illustrate the extreme sanctity of a holy person or to remind complacent mortals that He was the ultimate arbiter of everything, natural and unnatural, that occurred in the world. The modern worldview can only explain the magically inexplicable by saying that we just don't yet know the scientific explanation. This difference in worldviews means that there was much more space for discussion of the magical and supernatural in the prescientific era, because it was always open to interpretation whether an uncanny event was God's work or the Devil's, whether a magician might be a holy man or a witch, or just a madman.

Shakespeare's depiction of the supernatural and of magic and its practitioners draws on all levels of contemporary belief. There are ugly old witches, beautiful fairy queens and kings, ceremonial magicians who renounce their magic in order to (re)claim their political status, wizardly warriors, changelings, spells from books and chants from oral tradition. A few interesting themes emerge, however. Magic is associated especially with the Celts, both Welsh and Scottish. More generally, magic is something that is native to Someplace Else, whether Wales or Scotland—the "other" parts of the newly unified Britain—an island in the West Indies—the edge of the known world at the time—or the forest—the wilderness that lies beyond the comforts and familiarities of home. Good magic is practiced by attractive people, bad magic by ugly one. Male magic is more likely to derive from books, female magic from demons.

This dichotomy between (male) ceremonial magic and (female) practical magic became increasingly important in the subsequent centuries when, under the influence of the Enlightenment and the Industrial Revolution, the first acquired prestige through its similarity to experimental science and the second came to be regarded as quaint but ultimately harmless folklore.

CHAPTER 7

WHO NEEDS MAGIC?

THERE ARE ALMOST AS MANY THEORIES about why the witch hunts stopped as there are for why they happened in the first place. Once again, this is probably a case in which there are a number of reasons, rather than just once, and different reasons apply in different areas. The general explanation offered is some kind of increase in rationalism and a corresponding decline in the hold of religion over scholarship and intellectual life.

Yet the Hungarian historian Gábor Klaniczay (1990) has demonstrated that in the eighteenth century in the area governed by the Habsburg monarchy, the decline in a belief in witches was not so much a sign of an increase in "rationality" as a shift to belief in vampires as the cause of bad luck and unexplained ill health and death. Witchcraft trials in general had come late to Hungary, only beginning in the 1550s, and true witch panics did not occur until the 1720s and 1730s, when witch trials had almost ceased in Western Europe. The empress Maria Theresa enacted a series of laws that made it almost impossible to convict someone of seriously supernatural witchcraft and only punished the intent to harm or the real harming of other people and their property, in terms very similar to the witchcraft legislation of Henry VIII in England some two centuries earlier. The primary mover behind Maria Theresa's interest in eradicating witch beliefs was her court doctor and advisor Conrad van Sweiten, who wrote treatises on both witchcraft and vampirism as psychological disorders. This again seems to illustrate the enormous influence one or two powerful people may have on whether witch manias developed.

But even more to the point, witches were somewhat old hat in the European court of opinion by the mid-eighteenth century. Another reason for the decline in witch hunts seems to have been, if you will pardon the expression, sheer burn-out. There was a degree to which the witch hunts really were a kind of madness, when paranoia and terror and uncertainty made almost anything seem possible, even spirit flight and intercourse with the Devil, but nearly every witch hunt ended when the accusations went just one step too far and people's suspended disbelief fell heavily to earth. Nonetheless, there always seems to be a source of both magic and evil that lies just over the horizon, whether it is a witches' coven, an international Communist conspiracy, the Bilderberg Group, the papacy, or cannibals. To much of Europe in the eighteenth century, when witches no longer served as scapegoats for everything that went wrong in the world, vampires "presented the effects of harmful magical power in new and exciting terms for the people of that era" (Klaniczay 1990, p. 185). Furthermore, by laying these inexplicablities at the feet of the dead, the dangers of falsely accusing one's neighbors were avoided.

As Klaniczay points out, vampires inverted the natural order in virtually the same way that witches did:

> As for the religious polemicists, vampire beliefs represented a serious challenge, for they were forced to recognize in them the blasphemous reversal of some crucial Christian dogmas and cults. The vampire belief touched upon Christian ideas about resurrection. The vampire, like the Christian saint, was also a "very special dead"... whose corpse resisted decay, whose grave radiated a special light, whose fingernails and hair kept growing—like those of several medieval saints, e.g. Saint Oswald, Saint Edmund, and Saint Olaf ... thus demonstrating the persistence of

vital energy beyond death. The apparitions of vampires and the miracles connected with them were, in a way, negative reflections of the attributes of saints. And as for the most haunting capacity of the vampire, the bloodsucking—not only can one account for it in terms of the history of sacrificial blood...but one could also see it as a reversal of its Christianized version, the holy communion, which was depicted by late medieval and early modern mystics as a highly tangible bodily and material absorption of Christ's flesh and (more significantly) blood.... (ibid., p. 181)

What is interesting about this switch from a fascination with witches to one with vampires is that while both challenge and invert Christianity, each monster preys on different types of fear. The evil of the diabolical witch is in her corrupted soul, as evidenced by her worship of Satan rather than God, while the evil of the vampire is in its corrupted flesh. Both, however, become expressed through a morbidly fascinating sexuality: the witch's copulation with the Devil at her ecstatic Sabbath, the vampire's erotic "kiss." Even so, Satan is the sexual aggressor toward the human witch, while the vampire is the sexual aggressor against his human victim.

Another attraction of vampires was that they were a belief not just of peasants, but the peasants of the most "backward" areas of Europe. To sophisticates in the cities of Western Europe, vampires were good to think with because they weren't likely to show up on your doorstep asking to borrow a cup of flour and cursing you when you refused. Vampires were creatures of folklore, an area of scholarship that only began to formulate in the mid-seventeenth century. One of the earliest British folklorists was biographer and antiquarian John Aubrey (1626-1697), who looked around himself after the restoration of Charles II to the throne of Britain and realized that the experience of the Civil War and the Commonwealth had created a very different world from the one in which he had spent his childhood. One of the Puritans' aims had been to eliminate religious "superstition," which in many cases meant the elimination of tradition. After two decades without celebrating traditional holidays in the traditional ways, old customs had been forgotten or gone rusty.

Aubrey, in his *Miscellanies* (1696), *Remaines of Gentilisme and Judaisme* (not published until 1881), and other works, wrote down as much as he could remember, and as much as he could get other people to remember, of this world that he feared had forever vanished: beliefs, customs, traditions, lore of places, and anything else that came across his plate. From the very beginning, folklore was a discipline that conceived of itself as preserving something that was always on the verge of vanishing. And yet, in the twenty-first century, there is still folklore to be collected. Part of the definition of folklore is that it is forever not quite dead. Much like vampires.

The eighteenth and nineteenth centuries saw a return of the conceptual dichotomy between "my religion" and "your superstition." It may be that one of the contributing factors to witch mania was that the gap between "you" and "me" was so small that the minuscule became macrocosmic. Everyone in Europe was, by this time, Christian, and their differences of religious opinion were, in the grand scheme of things, minor. Even the differences that arose between Protestants and Catholics were largely organizational and interpretative; both religions still referred back to the same bible and the same Jesus and were closer to each other than even to Judaism. In the same way that staring at small grains of sand makes everything else seem enormous when you look up, the fine distinctions between elite and folk religion began to seem as enormous as the distinction between human and demon.

As Europeans began to explore and colonize the New World, Africa, and India, the distinctions between "us" and "them" became greater. Rather than differentiating based on beliefs about the degree of Jesus's divinity or one's opinions on clerical celibacy, "we" were white and "they" were dark, "we" were Christian and "they" were some kind of polytheistic savage, "we" wore proper clothes and "they" pranced about half-naked, "we" built enormous, magnificent sailing ships and "they" paddled canoes, "we" had guns and "they" had bows and arrows. Not only did Europeans seek to expand their political domination over larger and larger areas of land, not only did they seek to exploit the natural resources of that land, but they also (generously, in their opinion) sought to save the souls of all those savages by converting them to Christianity.

Europeans thus started to define "us" as Christian versus "them" as pagans, but the technological contrasts between European civilization and many of the tribal peoples they encountered, especially in Africa and the New World, made them also define "our" understanding of the workings of the world as scientific while "their" understanding was superstitious. Increasingly, then, it became possible to associate Christianity with rationalism and science on the one hand, and all nonbiblical religions with superstition and magic on the other.

The slow adoption of the theory of evolution, and its sociological adaptation as Social Darwinism, equated middle- and upper-class European children, non-European adults, and rural Europeans as inhabiting the same lower rung on the social-evolutionary ladder. As the distinction between "us" and "them" widened under exposure to the inhabitants of whole new continents, the differences between elite and folk culture, especially elite and folk religion, in Europe also came to seem less threatening, indeed, downright interesting. By the 1890s, it was possible for Lady Alice Gomme to suggest with barely a hint of scandal, in her studies of British children's singing games, that the song "London Bridge Is Falling Down" carries the faint echo of human sacrifice made to ensure the firmness of the bridge's foundation. In some parts of Europe two hundred years earlier, such a suggestion could have led to the singers being tortured and executed as Devil worshipers.

In 1736, James I's witchcraft statute was repealed in Great Britain, part of a general trend throughout Europe to overturn the laws of the witch hunt era. The Dutch Republic was the first European nation to end witch trials, where the last was held in 1659; Spain was the last to prosecute witches, with the last trial held in 1820. The bulk of the trials ceased in the middle fifty years of the 1700s. The general consensus was slowly shifting to disbelief in diabolical witchcraft; the concept of selling one's soul to Satan in return for magical powers as a real possibility was viewed with increasing skepticism, although as a literary trope it received one of its most powerful formulations in the early nineteenth century in Goethe's *Faust* (which will be discussed in the next chapter).

The 1736 witchcraft statute not only forbade prosecuting people for practicing witchcraft, sorcery, enchantment, and conjuration, but also made it a crime to claim to practice any type of magic. Any person who "pretend[ed] to exercise or use any kind of Witchcraft, Sorcery, Inchantment, or Conjuration, or undertake to tell Fortunes, or pretend, from his or her Skill or Knowledge in any occult or crafty Science, to discover where or in what manner any Goods or Chattels, supposed to have been stolen or lost, may be found" was subject to a year's imprisonment and exposure on the pillory for an hour once every three months during that time, as well as a fine at the judge's discretion. Legal opinion had returned to the early medieval stance that magic was impossible, and therefore any claim of its practice constituted fraud.

The decline in the belief in diabolical witchcraft coincided with the general decline in a belief in supernatural activity in the world, whether by demons, fairies, angels, even saints. Two cultural trends encouraged this decline: the general intellectual movement known as the Enlightenment and the increase in scientific investigation and discovery that accompanied it. The medieval and early modern worldview had been based on the concept of an orderly universe designed, and only completely understandable, by God. The more science revealed of the workings of the natural world, however, the more it appeared that human understanding was also potentially capable of completely understanding it. God and the supernatural in general were less necessary as an ultimate explanation. Nonetheless, even in the seventeenth century, early scientific investigators were careful to construct their alchemical/chemical apparatuses so that, for instance, all angles turned toward the right rather than the more sinister left, even when this created more awkward or excessively elaborate set-ups. This was not a case of a conversion experience and complete change of mindset from religion and superstition to science.

While belief in diabolical witchcraft came and went, folk magical practices continued, performed by both layfolk and magical professionals. They were folk medical practitioners, finders of lost and stolen objects, purveyors of love potions, midwives and abortionists, and readers of omens—just as they had always been. People were still anxious to ward off evil, whether from the ill intentions of neighbors or from indefinable bad luck. They were especially concerned to protect their houses, barns, and livestock. Archaeological remains of these folk magical practices turn up periodically, especially when old buildings are being torn down or renovated; archaeologist Ralph Merrifield made a specialization of collecting and analyzing these remains of ritual practice and it is possible to see enormous continuity from the Iron Age to the Industrial Age in the ways people hedged their bets against bad luck in even the most skeptical eras (Merrifield 1987; see also http://www.folkmagic.co.uk/).

Common magical practices included the hiding of objects within a house's walls, thresholds, and chimneys. So-called witch bottles were buried on house thresholds or under their hearths—entrances and exits to the building. Some of the bottles that have been discovered, usually in the course of renovation, are plain glass, but others are of a type called bellarmine, stoneware containers which have faces imprinted on them. Witch bottles usually contained human hair, sharp objects such as iron needles, pins, and nails, thorns, and sometimes pieces of fabric cut into the shape of a heart as well as urine. These may have been placed as apotropaic (evil-averting) charms to prevent witches from entering the house and attacking its inhabitants, or they may have been intended to counter-curse witches. Folk beliefs recorded up through the nineteenth century held that one way to identify a witch was to boil the cursed person's urine along with sharp objects and sometimes salt; the connection formed between witch and victim would then work in reverse, preventing the witch herself from urinating and thus putting her in untold torment. This would force the witch to come and beg her victim to release her from the counterspell, the price of which, naturally, was her lifting of her original curse.

Horse skulls are also found under hearths and floors. The reason for this practice is unclear. The most frequently stated purpose was that these skulls—as well as empty pots, which are also often found in the same places—made better acoustics inside churches and other places where people spoke in public or performed music. The ancient Greeks had discovered that bronze kettles placed underneath the seats of their outdoor ampitheaters would resonate with the tones of the actors's voices. Clay pots had similar resonant properties—not as good as bronze but cheaper—and were often used in medieval churches. In Scandinavia, horses' skulls and iron pots were used underneath floors on which grain was threshed to make the floor "sing" and in Ireland horses' skulls were buried under threshing floors, church floors, and the floors of houses where people gathered to play music both to improve the acoustics and for luck. A Swedish folklorist conducted experiments to prove that horses' skulls did, indeed, improve the echoing qualities and elasticity of floors. The question remains, however, how it was discovered that burying skulls underneath a floor had this property, and furthermore, why should people desire a "singing" floor? Merrifield suggests that the acoustic explanation is a rationalization of the practice, a side-effect of ritual burial of the heads of, most likely, sacrificial victims.

Dead, naturally mummified cats are also often found secreted within house walls in positions and places that suggest they were deliberately placed there, often in hunting stances with bodies of mice or rats under their feet or in their mouths. It may be that the evil to be averted was common vermin rather than witches, but cats' connection with witchcraft and the supernatural may mean that these cat corpses were thought to avert spiritual vermin—witches, after all, were often thought to travel about in the shape of mice, rats, and other small animals often hunted by cats.

The most common ritual object discovered in houses is a shoe, usually placed on a ledge within the chimney. The purpose of the shoe deposition is unknown, but the close association of a shoe with its wearer may well underlie whatever magic was intended. Shoes are mentioned in folklore as appropriate containers for entrapped demons and other malicious spirits, so the shoes in the walls may have been placed as spirit traps, just as the dead cats may have been supernatural mousetraps. The Freudian symbolism of the shoe as a metaphor for the vagina may connect these walled-in shoes with the Irish figure of the sheila-na-gig, a bas-relief sculpture of an ugly, aged woman, usually with a skull-like head and scrawny, sagging breasts, reaching down to expose and hold open her vagina.

Sheilas are most often discovered placed above doors or windows, especially of churches. The sheila has been described as a type of "erotic" sculpture (it is difficult to imagine anything less sexually arousing) or, somewhat more reasonably, as a pagan Irish fertility goddess (in which case, what is she doing on all those Christian churches?). Throughout European folklore, however, exposing one's genitals is an apotropaic gesture, a way of scaring away evil with the power of generativity (always a good thing). Amulets to ward off the Evil Eye, for instance, are usually very attractive, shiny, colorful items that are supposed to distract the Evil Eye from a vulnerable human to a fascinating but inert piece of jewelry. One of the more common Italian anti-Evil-Eye amulets is in the shape of a penis, and the fact of the matter is that naked genitals are distracting under just about any circumstances. Although the sheila might be scaring away demons with her flashing, it could also be that, like the vaginal shoe, she becomes a trap for the evil spirit attempting to enter the holy place.

Renovation also often exposes marks on interior beams that appear to have some magical, apotropaic purpose. These are quite different from marks that were made to ensure that the beams were put together in the proper order. Many of these marks look like "W"s, "M"s, and "V"s, perhaps to invoke the blessing of the Virgin Mary. Written charms, which unlike the dead cats, shoes, and witch bottles were probably prepared by professional cunning folk, have been found in houses and barns. These are usually written on paper and thus very few survive over long periods of time, but their content in many ways is in a direct line of descent from the lead-inscribed charms that date from the Roman era. Although these charms are generally blessings on the inhabitants rather than curses, they show the same kind of mixture of Latinate gibberish and quasi-mystical diagrams, especially utilizing astrological symbols.

Although protective and divinatory practices had enormous continuity from the Iron Age to the modern era, the more shamanic aspects of folk magic had been almost eradicated by witch mania. Trances led to dangerous things like believing you had flown to Bald Mountain to have sex with Satan. Groups such as the Friulian *bendantanti* had been convinced by the Inquisition that they were witches rather than witch-fighters. Shamanistic aspects of folk religion lingered longest in areas of eastern Europe such as Hungary, where the relatively late onset and rapid eclipse of witch mania diminished its long-term effects. The folklore of fairies and witches in

Hungary, Romania, Croatia, Slovenia, and surrounding areas has been analyzed by Éva Pócs (1989, 1999) and seems to show that fairies are conceived as the ancestral dead, in communication with mortal shamanic wizards, while witches primarily steal crops by mystical means. Pócs suggests that the concept of the witches' sabbath, involving trance flight and otherworldly feasting, was a displacement of the shamanic wizards' journeys to communicate with the fairy ancestors onto the diabolical, fertility-stealing witches under the influence of the elite beliefs of the Church, which effectively erased all the fine distinctions of folk belief.

Pócs points out that the diabolical, Devil-worshiping witch was a figure who existed purely in the world of belief and was, ironically enough, a relatively modern invention. In Eastern Europe, however, "we can also establish that there is an archaic type of witch, from which we can come to the common root of certain seers, magicians, and European witches" (Pócs 1999, p. 109). These healing "witches" were the descendants of the shamanic wizards who communicated with the Otherworld, not of witches per se. In trying to understand the roots of modern folklore, one feature that distinguishes healing magicians from diabolical witches is that the former are invariably born to their calling—marked physically by being born with a caul, hair, or teeth, for instance, or marked temporally by being born on Christmas or New Year's Day—while diabolical witches by definition acquired their power by selling their souls to Satan. Like the women condemned in early medieval penitentials for believing that they left their bodies at night to follow Herodias, Diana, or Holde, these Slavic "witches" did indeed worship a divine female even though, under the influence of Christianity, she might no longer be called a goddess.

These more remote areas of Europe provide a framework for understanding the varieties of folk magic that were obliterated elsewhere in Europe and also, by seeing what was lost, for understanding the new forms of belief that arose to fill the needs formerly addressed by shamanic magicians. The primary role of the shaman is to communicate with spirits. This function was partly filled in Western Europe by the type of cunning folk who had visions that revealed the location of missing objects, but the means of communicating with the dead was cut off. In 1848, however, the veil between the worlds began to lift.

The Fox sisters, Margarett and Kate, of Hydesville, New York, initiated the spiritualist movement when they began hearing raps in the wall of their home. They started rapping back, and a communication system evolved, with one knock for "yes," two for "no," and letters indicated by their numerical order in the alphabet (lucky that "z" is such an infrequent letter in English). The invisible entity identified itself as the spirit of Charles Haynes, a murder victim buried in the basement of the rented home. Whether the Foxes or any of the other mediums who materialized in their wake had any real contact with the spirits of the dead is very much a matter of opinion. People who believe in spiritualism focus on the instances that cannot be proved as fakes, and those who do not believe in spirits focus on the many cases of attested fraud.

Shamans had usually communicated with a kind of generic ancestral dead who offered wisdom and guidance for the group as a whole rather than specific messages for individuals. The accouterments of a spiritualist seance, however, came to include communications with the spirits of named individuals who essentially dropped in to chat by means of rapping, automatic writing (handwriting composed in a trance state), planchettes (a device that held a pencil and was "driven" by the combined psychic force of a group of people lightly touching the device with the tips of their fingers) ouija boards (where the planchette did not write, but pointed at pre-set letters on a board), possession of the very body of the medium in order to speak through him or her, and even materializing in the form of semi-opaque, semi-solid ectoplasm. While the manifestation of these spirits might be astonishing—the most renowned spiritualist mediums put on quite a show, with ectoplasmic spirits playing musical instruments while the medium was tied up to prove absence of fraud—the messages the spirits conveyed were usually quite banal. It was like getting a postcard from the Otherworld that just said "Having a wonderful time, wish you were here."

What mediums and shamans had in common, beyond communication with the Beyond, was a tendency towards tricksterism. Just as shamans are often accused of faking their healing activities by, for instance, appearing to pull a piece of bloody flesh out of a patient's body and claiming it is the source of the illness when, in fact, the shaman performed a sleight-of-hand trick, so mediums were often discovered by skeptical seance participants to have slipped, Houdini-like, from their ropes to play instruments, to have constructed "ectoplasmic" apparitions out of gauze and wires, to have thrown their voices, to have pushed planchettes, and so on. (See Hanson 2001, pp. 170-173 for some comparisons; Oppenheim 1985 provides an overview of mediums of all degrees of respectability operating in Britain in the nineteenth century.) Certainly spiritualism offered ample opportunity for con artists of all stripes to exercise their arts, but as some of the less judgmental researchers have noted, the expectations of ever bigger and more impressive effects produced on demand almost required fakery of anyone who might have begun with some authentic shamanic talent.

One of the most well-respected mediums of the nineteenth century was Daniel Dunglas Home (1833-1886), a man whose activities seemed least likely to have been faked. In many ways, his seances were typical:

> He frequently fell into a state of trance prior to making contact with the spirits.... In Home's presence, furniture trembled, swayed, and rose from the floor (often without disturbing the objects on its surface); diverse articles soared through the air; the seance room itself might appear to shake with quivering vibrations; raps announced the arrival of the communicating spirits; spirit arms and hands emerged, occasionally to write messages or distribute favors to the sitters; musical instruments, particularly Home's celebrated accordion, produced their own music; spirit voiced uttered their pronouncements; spirit lights twinkled, and cool breezes chilled the sitters.... Their clothing might be pulled by playful spirits; they might even be poked and pinched (Oppenheim 1985, p. 13).

Home's more remarkable talents included levitation—on one apparently impeccably witnessed occasion, he walked out of an upper-story window and walked back in a window in another room—the handling of live coals, and an ability to stretch his body by as much as a foot in length. These are all skills associated with shamanism. Home was also unusual among nineteenth century mediums in his willingness to conduct his seances in relatively well-lit conditions. Most mediums insisted on conducting their seances in near pitch dark, conditions that could hide a multitude of sins, fakes, frauds, and tricks.

Whether real or fake, spiritualism provided a very modernist take on contact with the Otherworld. Content was not important; the mere fact of contact was what provided hope and satisfaction to the medium's clients. The more tangible the contact, the better. The criteria for "reality" were based in science rather than metaphysics: things that could be seen, heard, smelled, or best of all touched. There was a vogue for "spirit photographs" that appeared to show the dearly departed hovering protectively over their loved ones; the new and nearly magical technology of photography appeared to offer positive proof of spirit life until the mysteries of double exposures—accidental or deliberate—became common knowledge. Essentially, all the spirit had to do was show up; science would provide the meaning and the message.

As spiritualism worked its way into the edges of the mainstream, part of the interest and excitement of contact with spirits was the possibility that some definitive proof of life after death was imminent. Groups such as the Society for Psychical Research hoped, through their work, to answer questions about the relationship of the mind and the body. Many scientists felt compelled to give spiritualism serious consideration just in case there was something to it that could open new vistas in psychology or physics. Others were openly partisan. Alfred Russel Wallace, who conceived of the theory of natural selection independently of Charles Darwin, was an ardent spiritualist and exempted the human mind—and by extension the human soul—from the purely materialistic operation of evolution. Wallace was inclined to see in spiritualism the key to all those aspects of the human species that appeared to set us apart from the rest of the animal world (Oppenheim 1985, pp. 267-325). Spirits were valuable in their ability to provide evidence about the nature of life on earth.

This is perhaps the most important difference between shamanism and spiritualism. Shamanism is based on a belief that the spirit world, the Otherworld, has an almost magnetic attraction for the incorporeal aspect of the human being, drawing the spirit out of the physical body and trapping it. Shamans' power is evidenced by their ability to come and go from the spirit world at will, evading the traps and rescuing less powerful souls. Shamans also go to the spirit world to gain the spirits' knowledge and bring it back to the physical world. Even so, living human spirits are the dumb guys in the spirit world. Everything flows in the opposite direction in spiritualism. Dead souls come back to the physical world and manifest themselves in as physical a state as incorporeal entities can manage. The medium is the magnet that draws them here, sometimes even against their will. The notion that spirits could provide information on missing wills, hidden treasure, or even misplaced glasses (also a specialization of cunning folk) was always an enticing prospect, but there seem to be no instances of this kind of useful information actually being offered; it is a classic instance of something that only happens to a friend-of-a-friend. The spirits did not seem particularly interested in conducting anthropological fieldwork on the afterlife and communicating their findings to the Society for Psychical Research.

Although many spiritualists were at least nominally Christian, the movement also attracted people whose faith was shaky or even absent. The materialist, scientific facet of the spirit world made it possible to believe in an afterlife that did not consist solely of sitting at the right hand of Jehovah. Heaven began to acquire nondenominational parameters. In addition to the soft-focus happiness and comfort offered by spirits contacted through seances, the Orientalizing influence of Theosophy also colored the changing view of the Otherworld, its denizens, and those who communicated with them that emerged in the course of the nineteenth century.

Theosophy was the discovery, invention, or fabrication (depending on your point of view) of Madame Helena Blavatsky, a rather dumpy Russian woman of overwhelming charisma who claimed to have sojourned with the "ascended masters" or "mahatmas" in the mysterious and then virtually unexplored (by Europeans) mountains of Tibet. Blavatsky claimed to have learned essentially shamanic procedures for accessing alternate levels of reality, spiritual planes from which beings infinitely wiser, older, and more incorporeal than humans—daimons, perhaps?—worked to maintain cosmic balance. Here were kept the "Akashic records" of everything that ever had happened or ever would happen. Unlike seance spirits, Blavatsky communicated what she learned in the spirit world at length: her major theoretical works, *Isis Unveiled: A Master Key to the Mysteries of Ancient and Modern Science and Theology* (1877) and *The Secret Doctrine: The Synthesis of Science, Religion, and Philosophy* (1888), run to some three thousand pages in total, and her collected works comprise sixteen volumes.

Blavatsky led a peripatetic childhood as the daughter of a Russian military man and, when her marriage to an older man when she was seventeen did not work out, she spent some twenty-five years traveling the world following a variety of exotic occupations—at least, according to her own story. Her habit of embroidering stories over time made it difficult to pick out their underlying basis in fact. Wherever she had been, Blavatsky arrived in New York in 1873 and, in alliance with Henry Olcott, a lawyer, journalist, and politician, created her own religion, which she called Theosophy. Her aim was to elucidate the underlying unity of all world religions, establishing the tradition of claiming that all great holy men (and women) of the ages preached essentially the same message of peace, love, and understanding. In particular, she emphasized similarities between Christianity, Buddhism, and Hinduism, participating in the tradition that Jesus's "lost years" were spent in Central Asia, where he absorbed the wisdom of the mystic East which he then transmitted to the Middle East, and thence to the rest of the world.

In addition to Eastern mysticism, Blavatsky eventually drew upon the Western esoteric tradition of the Freemasons, the Rosicrucians, the Knights Templar, as well as others who have become the stuff of modern conspiracy theory. She posited a world that was run by infinitely wise beings who were not gods but humans who advanced to ever higher levels of being through study, open-mindedness to alternate realities, and contact with otherworldly beings. Blavatsky was constantly dogged by allegations of fraud and trickery, like other mediums, like shamans, like all tricksters—she is unusual in being one of the few women to embody this archetype, and much of the outrage she caused was as much due to her flouting of conventional female roles as her mischievous occultism:

... [S]he looked overall like a badly wrapped and glittering parcel. She talked incessantly in a guttural voice, sometimes wittily and sometimes crudely. She was indifferent to sex yet frank and open about it; fonder of animals than of people; unsnobbish, unpretentious, scandalous, capricious, and rather noisy. She was also humorous, vulgar, impulsive, and warmhearted, and she didn't give a hoot for anyone or anything (Washington 1993, p. 41).

Perhaps one of the more remarkable things about Blavatsky's career is that she was *not* considered to be a witch. It is hard to imagine anyone making her claims in the seventeenth century without being executed promptly as a self-confessed witch. Her "masters" would have been labeled the Devil and his minions, her theology of a Mother Goddess espoused in *Isis Unveiled* would have rung alarm bells in minds familiar with texts prescribing penances for believing in following Diana and Herodias, and it would have been taken for granted that any non-Christian church could practice nothing but Devil-worship. Yet Madame Blavatsky was never viewed as anything worse than a trickster, and there were many people who considered her authentically holy.

Between Theosophy, spiritualism, and similar movements, the nineteenth century saw an increasing acceptance of the idea that the world contained more levels of reality and more types of inhabitants than simply humans on one level, God and the angels on the side of the supernatural good, and Satan and demons on the side of supernatural evil. The spirits who possessed mediums might be faked, but they were not evil (not in reality; fiction was another matter). The "masters" or "mahatmas," adopting Buddhist tradition, might willingly accept human birth to guide less advanced mortals, and humans might eventually, over numerous lives, acquire enough wisdom and mastery to become mahatmas themselves.

What Blavatsky specifically did not do was practice magic. Her powers were completely natural, whether one took the attitude that they were natural trickery or believed that she had access to aspects of nature beyond the reach of the hoi polloi. Magic had its students, however. One of the most prominent magical groups of the nineteenth and early twentieth century was the Hermetic Order of the

Golden Dawn, founded in 1888 and dedicated to the practice of ritual magic. This descended from the scholarly magical investigations of medieval and Renaissance alchemists, Kabbalists, and Hermeticists. The four founding members, William Robert Woodman, William Wynn Westcott, Samuel Liddell Mathers (later known as Macgregor Mathers), and Alphonsus F. A. Woodward, had backgrounds in Freemasonry, Rosicrucianism, Theosophy, the Hermetic Society, and other occult groups. The Golden Dawn was an unusually influential organization that attracted many members of the more bohemian elements of society—perhaps its most famous member was the poet William Butler Yeats. As Ronald Hutton notes:

> It needs to be emphasized how remarkable an organization Westcott and Mathers had constructed. In its structure it resembled the Societas Rosicruciana and the Freemasonry upon which the latter had been based, having a graded process of initiation, with accompanying ceremonies, robes, and symbolic tools. Instead of lodges, it had temples.... In its attitude to religion and gender, however, it deliberately adopted the open-door policy of the Theosophical Society. Westcott taught neophytes of the new order to regard it as a companion to Theosophy .... He emphasized the major role of women in occult researches .... The process of training represented by the five grades of the outer group was remarkably thorough and intense, furnishing a grounding in the main Hebrew, Greek, Graeco-Egyptian, medieval, and early modern esoteric traditions, and the accompanying ceremonies represented a blend of all these (Hutton 1999, pp. 76-77).

Golden Dawn rituals involved invoking and banishing elemental spirits of directions and the use of working tools (cup, pentacle, dagger, and wand). The basic levels of magical working invoked a powerful divine female figure—Isis-Urania—and her male consort—Pan. Their magic mixed the traditional magical goals of ritual magic, such as personal empowerment, enrichment, attraction of love, with a focus on mystical union with the divine,

> bringing [the magician] closer to spiritual maturity and potency, by inflaming the imagination, providing access to altered states of con-

sciousness, and strengthening and focusing will-power. It was a therapy designed to enable human beings to evolve further into deities, to bring forth the divinity already within them ... In the last analysis, it did not matter to this work whether or not the entities concerned had any actual existence as long as the magician felt as if they did at the moment of working, and achieved the transforming visions and sensations which were the object of the process (Hutton 1999, p. 82-83).

By the end of the nineteenth century, then, there were two main streams of magical practice operating in Western Europe. On one hand was a folk magic whose goals can be generalized as healing—of humans, animals, and farmland—and visualization of the unseen— the future, lost or stolen objects, treasure. On the other hand was upper- and middle-class ritual magic, which had as its purpose the spiritual development of its participants and verged on religion.

Spiritualism, meanwhile, repeopled the immaterial world with ancestors—neither angel nor Devil nor demon nor daimon. Mediums communicated with the spirit world but now to transmit information to individuals rather than to the community as a whole. Rather than providing help in hunting for wildlife, the spirits provided help in hunting for misplaced paperwork and trinkets. The functions united in the figure of the archaic shaman, the ancient magician, or the medieval witch had become fragmented into cunning folk, ritual magicians, and mediums. Professionalization had hit magic.

CHAPTER 8

WITCHES ARE SO LAST CENTURY

In ADDITION TO THE RISE OF RATIONALISM, the eighteenth century also saw the rise of the novel. As witches were not of particularly central concern to the era, however, they did not figure to any significant degree in this emerging literary form. The earliest novels were concerned with events of the real and modern world; in *Don Quixote* (1605, 1615), for example, the Don's belief in magic and enchantment is both a sign of his madness and a result of his excessive reading of old-fashioned romances. A belief in magic is represented as typical of a medieval worldview in Cervantes' masterpiece.

Magic and its practitioners did not become relevant to the novel until the emergence of the Gothic genre in the late eighteenth century. As did Cervantes, the writers of Gothic novels used magic as a signifier of the medieval worldview they were attempting to invoke. Even so, Gothic novelists were more attracted to ghosts and vampires as representatives of medieval magic than they were in witchcraft. The first of the genre, Horace Walpole's *The Castle of Otranto* (1764), gets off to a ripping start with a prophecy of doom and the sickly young heir to the principate of Otranto crushed to death by a giant stone helmet that falls out of the sky, an image straight out of the opening credits of *Monty Python's Flying Circus*. The helmet is discovered to belong to a statue in a nearby church, and the hapless young man who points this out is accused of sorcery. Ghosts, ancestors delivering words of doom from within their portrait frames, more ghosts, portentous dreams, unearthly spectral moans, bleeding statues, ominous thunder on cue, and again more ghosts propel the narrative at breakneck pace to its melancholy conclusion.

Walpole originally published the novel under a pseudonym, passing off the narrative itself as a translation of an Italian text dating to 1529 discovered in the library of a northern English Catholic family. Within the context of Protestant, eighteenth century England, the events of the novel are removed in several ways: the story is ancient, rather than modern; the locale is Italy, rather than England; the characters are Catholic, rather than Anglican; causation is supernatural, rather than realistic. Although the basic concerns of the plot—the transfer of power in class relations, gender relations, generational relations, usurpation and tyranny, and so on—are completely relevant to real life, their representation in the novel takes place within a complete inversion of "normal" life.

Nearly all English Gothic novels had Catholic casts of characters and took place in the past and on the Continent. They epitomized everything that was "Other" to the Enlightenment English mind, unconsciously taking part in the traditional role of magic as an inversion of normality. One reason why witches per se may not have appeared with any frequency in these novels is that their presence would have demanded addressing the issue of human practice of magic; the magic of the Gothic novel was always inhuman or posthuman. Walpole never explains the means by which Alfonso's stone helmet squashed the unhappy Conrad at the opportune moment, or any of the other supernatural occurrences of his novel. They simply occur, because that's the kind of thing that happened in those benighted Catholic days. The villain of the piece, Manfred, is overbearing, unscrupulous, murderous, lecherous, and increasingly irrational, but he is always the victim of magic rather than its perpetrator. The supernatural intervenes to oust the unrightful prince, not to assist him in maintaining his hold on the throne.

One of the most notorious Gothic novels of its day was *The Monk* (1796) by Matthew Lewis. (Indeed, so notorious was the novel that Lewis came to be known as "Monk" Lewis after his magnum opus.) Although the protagonist of the novel is a monk rather than a witch, the novel revolves around the notion of selling one's soul to the Devil. Lewis claimed to have been inspired by the queen of the eighteenth century Gothic, Ann Radcliffe, but while Radcliffe was careful always to conclude her novels with a rational explanation for all the weird events of the preceding 700 or so pages (door hinges in need of oil, odd reflections in cobweb-draped mirrors grown dingy with the schmutz of the ages, secret passages, and so on), Lewis went straight to Hell for his motive agents.

The main character is the monk Ambrosio, a charismatic preacher who draws audiences from miles around Madrid. However, his inspiration is soon revealed to derive from vanity and pride rather than authentic piety, and his commitment to monkish chastity is the first thing to crumble. Ambrosio is seduced by a young monk named Rosario, who then reveals himself to be a young woman named Matilda, who later reveals herself to be a demon sent by the Devil himself to corrupt Ambrosio. In addition to his sexual cavortings with this ambiguously gendered and speciesed seducer, Ambrosio conceives an unholy obsession with the virginal Antonia, whom he rapes and murders after murdering her mother Elvira to get his hands on Antonia; then he discovers that Elvira was in fact his long-lost mother, so he has committed not only rape and murder but also incest and matricide. Accused of sorcery as well as rape and murder, imprisoned and tortured by the Inquisition (for he can only maintain his facade of piety for so long with all these heinous distractions), Ambrosio signs his soul over to the Devil in return for release, but the Devil, ever a stickler for details and the letter of the law, removes him from the prison and then, once outside, drops him to his death onto jagged rocks from an enormous height. There he lingers for six days, tormented by thirst, insect stings, and eagles picking at his mangled flesh, until a torrential rain washes him into a river and his soul departs for its eternal damnation in Hell.

The Castle of Otranto used Catholicism as a convenient shorthand for the "superstitious" mental outlook that accepted the occurrence of supernatural events. *The Monk*, however, makes its connection between Catholicism and Devil-worship explicit. Ambrosio falls because he is a monk who has abnormal expectations of piety and chastity laid upon him. His talents make him a natural mark for the Devil's attention—much as the Evil Eye is attracted to anything exceptionally pretty or perfect—and his human nature preordains that he will fall to temptation. (The eighteenth century, like the twenty-first, was very suspicious about what clerical celibacy could lead to.) Once he has Ambrosio in his clutches, Lucifer exults,

> Tremble, abandoned hypocrite! Inhuman parricide! Incestuous rav-isher! Tremble at the extent of your offences! And you it was who thought yourself proof against temptation, absolved from human frailties, and from error and vice! Is pride then a virtue? Is inhumanity no fault? Know, vain man! That I long have marked you for my prey: I watched the movements of your heart; I saw that you were virtuous from vanity, not principle, and I seized the fit moment of seduction. I observed your blind idolatry of the Madonna's picture. I bade a subordinate but crafty spirit assume a similar form, and you eagerly yielded to the blandishments of Matilda! (Lewis 1796/1952, p. 418).

Amrbosio's Achilles' heel is thus his worship of the Virgin Mary, his devotion to a divine female leading inevitably to his seduction by the forces of Satan. Mariolatry (worship of the Virgin Mary) was an aspect of Catholicism that made eighteenth century Protestants extremely uneasy, and Lewis's description of Ambrosio's devotion as "idolatrous" was nothing unusual in his day and age. The Church is presented as a breeding ground for hypocrisy, and although Ambrosio is certainly responsible for the crimes he commits, there is also a sense that the "unnaturalness" of the life he is forced to lead amplifies any innate weaknesses he may have.

Both Matilda and Lucifer argue that Ambrosio should sell his soul because, with the crimes he has committed, he is going to go to Hell when he dies anyway, so why not at least spend his years of life in pleasure? Matilda, announcing that she has sold her soul in exchange for escape from the Inquisition, announces that,

I have sold distant and uncertain happiness for present and secure. I have preserved a life, which otherwise I had lost in torture; and I have obtained the power of procuring every bliss which can make that life delicious! The infernal spirits obey me as their sovereign; by their aid shall my days be passed in every refinement of luxury and voluptuousness. I will enjoy unrestrained the gratification of my senses; every passion shall be indulged even to satiety; then will I bid my servants invent new pleasures, to revive and stimulate my glutted appetites! I go impatient to exercise my newly gained dominion. I pant to be at liberty (Lewis 1796/ 1952, p. 408).

Although Lewis is not explicitly addressing the question of why so many people accused of witchcraft admitted to this "impossible" crime, he does advance here a rationalization for the admissions to witchcraft during the early modern era: what did these people have to lose? Although Lucifer most likely did not show up in the prison cells where accused witches were held and offer them the deal he makes to Ambrosio, it must have been very clear to many of these people that there was no way they were going to get out of this alive, so they might as well get it over with. They might not spend their remaining days in "luxury and voluptuousness," but at least the torture would stop. Ambrosio fell victim to Lucifer's final trick, however—the guard rattling the door, whose imminent entrance sealed Ambrosio's decision to sell his soul since death appeared to be on his doorstep, was in fact carrying his pardon.

The most famous tale of selling one's soul to the Devil, however, is that of Faust. There was a real Faust, mentioned in a letter of 1507 as a fool and charlatan; in 1543, a Protestant pastor in Basel, Switzerland, named Johann Gast claimed to have met Faust and asserted that the magician derived his power from a contract with the Devil. This forms the nucleus of the Faust legend, elements of which were first collected in the *Volksbuch* by Johann Speiss in 1587 and received its first dramatic representation in Christopher Marlowe's play *Doctor Faustus*, written about a year later. Marlowe's Faust deserved eternal damnation for meddling in affairs not fit for human consumption, but by the Romantic era, Faust became a representative of heroic human striving for knowledge in Johann Wolfgang von Goethe's dramatic poem *Faust* (1808).

At the beginning of the play, Faust is trying to use magic to understand the workings of the universe, with magic as a metaphor for natural science. He becomes suicidal as he realizes that he has spent his life in a pursuit of knowledge that can never be complete, and in the process has missed out on actual experience. When the Devil, Mephistopheles, appears to tempt him (as the result of a Jobian bet between himself and God), what he offers is not the traditional magical power for which medieval witches sold their souls, but physical pleasure, which will be created, aided, and abetted by magical means. In a significant switch from the traditional role of the witch as the servant of Satan, it is Mephistopheles who becomes Faust's servant; likewise, it is Mephistopheles who performs the magic, while Faust simply reaps its benefit.

The one aspect of Goethe's work that does retain traditional magical concerns is its focus on love. Faust has Mephistopheles use his magic to get him the woman he desires, Gretchen, even though Faust treats her badly once he has obtained her and she dies, shamed and imprisoned. Gretchen, however, goes immediately to heaven, even though she has inadvertently poisoned her mother, been the cause of her brother's death in a duel with Faust, and deliberately drowned her illegitimate baby. It would seem that it is her steadfastness in refusing Faust's offer to magically free her from prison that reveals her purity of soul, for even if she were acquitted of the deaths of her mother and brother, the murder of one's infant would inevitably be considered a damning act in medieval, and even Enlightenment Germany.

Faust's compact with Mephistopheles—signed in blood, in the best demonic style—requires that in return for Mephistopheles' service, Faust will lose his soul to Mephistopheles if the Devil can create for him one moment of perfect happiness (the gypsies in the television series *Buffy the Vampire Slayer* and *Angel* had obviously read their *Faust*, even if they had not quite thought it all the way through—a topic that will be discussed in chapter 10). Here, again, is a revision of the traditional Devil's compact: witches sold their souls for specific powers that they acquired immediately, so their souls were immediately forfeit, even if they were to die in the next instant (as Ambrosio discovered), whereas the deal between Faust and Mephistopheles is conditional. Faust gets all the benefit of Mephistopheles' magic and Mephistopheles can do anything he can think of to win the bet, but ultimately he has no control over Faust's subjective reaction to his efforts. Furthermore, the happiness clause is inserted at Faust's insistence, so that when, ultimately, Mephistopheles loses the deal, it is because the human, not the Devil, has manipulated the fine print.

Mephistopheles takes Faust to a witch to restore his youth. There is an interesting contrast, then, between the scholarly magician and the ugly crone. Faust asks, reasonably enough, why Mephistopheles cannot restore Faust's youth himself; surely the Devil should be powerful enough to perform such an act without having to rely on an ugly old woman to do the job for him. Mephistopheles replies that the potion takes a long time to ferment, and the witch happens to have some about, so even though the source of the knowledge is the Devil, the action and use of the potion, magical though it is, is still subject to the natural laws of brewing. This is in contrast to the previous scene, where Mephistopheles has conjured fine wines for the patrons of an alehouse.

In the witch's kitchen—a scene inspired by Shakespeare's *Macbeth*—Faust first asks about the purpose of a sieve, which turns out to be used for detecting thieves (the use of sieves for divination and the identification of thieves both being standard witches' skills) and then sees the image of the woman he is to love in a mirror (another traditional divination, although there are generally rituals that must first be performed before the image of the soon-to-be-beloved appears). The witch, when she arrives, does not at first recognize the Devil, for he has lost or hidden his horns, tail, and cloven hoof and changed his name from Satan to Mephistopheles. He is a modern, up-to-date Devil now, while the witch is living in the past, committing all the ancient crimes. She draws a magic circle and chants preparatory to administering the youth potion to Faust, but Mephistopheles, in an aside, assures the scholar that this is merely mumbo-jumbo, and the two men disparage the old woman's performance. The ritual is stage-dressing, while the real power lies in the brewing of the potion—the more "scientific" the magic, the more "real" it is. Witchcraft is clearly presented as old-fashioned and largely fraudulent, with a core of natural science in the parts that work dressed up to trick the credulous. The tricksy aspect is the part specific to the female witch's practice, while the male magician goes straight for the active ingredients.

When Gretchen is at her nadir, Mephistopheles attempts to distract Faust by taking him to the witches' sabbath on Walpurgisnacht (May Eve). This, again, is depicted in traditional terms of feasting and dancing on a mountaintop, with witches arriving by broom and goat-back. The A-list attendees include Baubo (the Greek demi-goddess who raised a laugh in the mourning Demeter by raising her skirt); Volund, or Wayland, the Germanic hero and smith-god; and Lilith, Adam's first wife turned baby-stealer. Less exalted participants include government officials, vendors of shoddy goods, and a "proctophantasmist" who is outraged at the fact that the witches do not conform to his theories. Faust is almost drawn in to the jollity, but his thoughts return to Gretchen when, as he is dancing with a beautiful woman, a red mouse emerges from her mouth (another typical witchy behavior, as the soul leaves, shamanically, through the mouth to do the witch's bidding) and draws his attention to an apparition that appears to be Gretchen. Mephistopheles' reaction to this is rather remarkable for the Devil: he tells Faust not to look at the apparition because it is a magical illusion.

The next distraction presented to Faust is a play-within-a-play called *Walpurgis-Night's Dream, or, Oberon and Titania's Golden Wedding Feast*, a direct reference to Shakespeare's *Midsummer Night's Dream*. The attendees in the play represent a spectrum of "demonic" characters, from fairies and witches to philosophers and scientists. This play is more of a masque, and serves more as an opportunity for social satire than magical commentary, but it repeats the theme of a "modern" magic existing alongside the older, more traditional (dare we say old-fashioned and out-of-date) variety.

Balanced on the fine line between the Enlightenment and the Romantic era, Goethe creates an inclusive vision of magic—demonic and otherwise—and seems to leave with a version of "the more things change, the more they stay the same." Goethe utilizes the folklore of witchcraft, magic, the witches' sabbath, the demonic contract, and many other aspects of traditional magic, but he inverts many of them and ends with, essentially, an inversion of Bishop Arnaud of Citaux's possibly apocryphal directive on massacring Cathars, "Kill them all. God will recognize his own." God indeed does recognize his own (Gretchen) no matter what sins were committed in life. The soul may be sold, but the Devil cannot claim it unless the seller himself changes his soul in a demonic direction. The medieval point of view regarded the soul as a mere chattel, and its goodness or badness depended entirely on the nature of its owner, which was not the human being but God or the Devil (an essentially feudal view of the soul that regarded it as a land-bound serf). Goethe sees the soul as something uniquely the property of a human being, an individual, who may sell it but who ultimately retains all responsibility for how good or how bad it becomes. The most the Devil can do is provide temptation.

At roughly the same time that Goethe was composing *Faust*, the Grimm brothers, Jakob and Wilhelm, were collecting oral German-language folktales, or *Märchen*. They published their first collection of eithy-six these tales under the title of *Kinder- und Hausmärchen* in 1812; the collection went through seven edition between 1812 and 1857 and ultimately contained two hundred folktales plus ten "children's legends." The Grimms were motivated by Romantic nationalism to preserve the "shattered jewels" (as they put it) of ancient Germanic mythology.

Folktales, they felt, preserved a nation's pure ethnic spirit, uncontaminated by elite-literary elements that circulated in the cosmopolitan arena of the city, where people of all nations and races interacted and picked up good stories that were not, in the ethnic sense, their own. The Grimms were collecting tales in a Germany that was not, at that time, a single political entity, but rather a messy conglomeration of principalities, city-states, dukedoms, and other miniscule polities that had just been thrown into even greater disarray by the Napoleonic Wars. The only thing that clearly defined German identity was the German language, and it is no coincidence that in addition to his work as a collector of contemporary folktales, Jakob Grimm was also a ground-breaking philologist, discovering several of the patterns of sound-shift that German had undergone in its development from primordial Indo-European.

The Grimm's attitudes toward ethnicity and nationalism seems rather naive from a multicultural postmodern perspective—in the twenty-first century, any mention of "ethnic purity" sets the alarm bells ringing wildly—and they also were not above editing the tales they heard in order to make them conform to their conception of a real folktale. Their informants were not all peasants, as they seemed to suggest; indeed one of their best storytellers, Marie Hassenpflug, came from a French-speaking family. The earlier the edition of their collection, the more earthy and vulgar the stories. Despite the fact that "fairy tales" soon came to be considered morally uplifting children's fare, the Grimms did not begin by collecting children's stories. When they realized that this was their audience, however, Wilhelm began editing the tales into more (allegedly) child-friendly form—references to sex between unwed lovers were elided, mean mothers became wicked stepmothers, and fathers with incestuous urges turned into devils. It was their seventh and last edition, and thus the most bowdlerized, that became the basis for nearly all of the translations, including Margaret Hunt's translation into English published in 1888.

The enormous popularity of the *Kinder- und Hausmärchen* ironically transcended the Grimm's initial intention of preserving specifically German folktales by making most of their tales truly international. "Cinderella," "Little Red Riding Hood," "The Frog Prince," "Sleeping Beauty," "Snow White," "Beauty and the Beast," "Rapunzel," "Hansel and Gretel," "The Brementown Musicians," "The Robber Bridegroom," "Rumpelstiltskin," "Snow White and Rose Red," all appear. As Western society became increasingly urbanized and village cunning folk were less and less part of people's everyday lives, as professional doctors took over the health care arena for both people and animals, police forces took over the detection of thieves and the recovery of missing objects, science developed means of ameliorating the extremes of uncertainty in farming, most people only encountered the image of the witch in folktales.

Folktale witches are closer to the imagined, demonic witches of the witch hunt era than to folk magical practitioners. Like evil witches dating back to the classical era, the primary goal of these witches is to threaten fertility, particularly vulnerable children. The witch in "Hansel and Gretel" is a case in point. At the beginning of the tale, the wicked stepmother encourages the children's father to abandon them so that there will be enough food for the adults—an inversion of the traditional woman's role of feeding everyone in the family before herself. However, her concern is to preserve her own life at the expense of the future generation; she does not want so much to thwart their fertility as to preserve her own. The witch, however, goes one step further in wanting to eat the children herself. Here the children are demoted to the level of livestock, to be fattened for slaughter. It is interesting, however, that in this tale that is so concerned with who gets enough to eat, it is Hansel who gets fattened in a cell while Gretel is fed crab shells and forced to work. It would seem that the only way for a female to get enough to eat in this folktale world is to feed on "forbidden" food—food that should go to the children, or the children themselves, and in the end, is there any difference?

While the witch in "Hansel and Gretel" threatens fertility in the aspect of children, who will become the parents of the future and ensure the continuance of the species, the witch in "Rapunzel" threatens fertility in two ways, first by taking advantage of a pregnant woman's cravings (again the issue is food, its nature, and how to get enough of it), and secondly by imprisoning a nubile young woman and preventing her from mating with a man and producing more children. Rapunzel's mother's cravings for the rampion in the witch's garden is life-threatening; if she doesn't get it, she will die and her baby with her. This is furthermore a particularly precious child, because the couple has been infertile so far. The witch, by claiming Rapunzel in exchange for the rampion, allows the mother to live, but effectively destroys the family's continuation into the next generation. As soon as Rapunzel reaches puberty, the witch shuts her away in the tower, and when the girl manages, despite all the obstacles the witch has put in the way, to have sex with a passing prince, it results in disaster for both of them: Rapunzel is exiled in the desert—the most infertile terrain on Earth— and the prince is blinded by thorns. The happy ending, however, is signified by Rapunzel giving birth to not one but two children, and the prince's eyes being healed by Rapunzel's tears—water in the desert initiating rebirth.

The Grimms were particularly interested in the remnants of pagan mythology that persisted in the oral tradition, and one of their tales, "Mother Holle," concerns a supernatural figure who is patently descended from the goddess Holde, one of the goddesses whom pagan women followed as they did Diana and Herodias as recorded (and condemned) in the early medieval penitentials. This Otherworldly female is good or bad only in reaction to human action. When a good girl finds herself in Holle's country—after falling through a well, so she has reached the underground spirit world—her spontaneously helpful and industrious behavior, such as taking bread out of the oven, shaking ripe apples off the tree, and keeping Holle's house clean and her comforter fluffed up, is rewarded with gold, while her lazy sister, who does as little work as possible and that only in hopes of reward, is covered in pitch.

This is an extremely didactic tale advancing a very conservative, traditional view of women's roles, so it is interesting that the agent of the moral is, in fact, a pagan goddess. Burchard of Worms, back in the tenth century, did not seem to be under the impression that deluded women believed they followed Herodias, Holde, Diana, or Perchte in order to keep their houses clean. Archaic shamans wafted to the Otherworld in ecstasy, not on Endust.

The folklorist Max Lüthi, in attempting to define the folktale as a genre, compared the attitude toward the supernatural in *märchen* versus in legends of various types. In legends, the Otherworld and its inhabitants are experienced as Other, even if that world is close, even coterminous, with the mortal realm. Encountering the supernatural raises a numinous frisson of fear and anxiety in humans, and they are aware that the mundane has gone out of whack. Legends are told "for the sake of what is strange or marvelous in the events described. Outstandingly good or outstandingly evil human beings are thought to be basically strange and unfathomable, and for this reason they are the subject of story after story" (Lüthi 1982, pp. 5-6).

In folktales, in contrast, the magical and supernatural are taken completely for granted. If an animal speaks in a legend, Lüthi points out, it is taken as a sign of portentous goings-on; if an animal speaks in a folktale, the hero reacts as though his neighbor bade him good day. Likewise, no matter when the hero may be given a magical object, he only really looks at it and uses it when it is necessary:

> In folktales the numinous excites neither fear nor curiosity.... [The hero] is afraid of dangers, not of the uncanny. Witches, dragons, and giants frighten him no more than human rogues and robbers. He avoids such creatures because they have the power to kill or injure, not because of their supernatural character.... To him, everything belongs in the same dimension (Lüthi 1982, pp. 6-7).

At the same time, the supernatural figures of legend exist alongside humans, inhabiting the abandoned and inaccessible spaces of the world, both physical, such as wastelands, forests, lakes, and rivers, and temporal, particularly nighttime. In folktales, however, the giants, ogres, and witches are encountered far away, when the hero or heroine leaves the familiar space of home and enters the world of adventure. "In legends otherworld beings are physically near human beings but spiritually far. In folktales they are far away geographically but near in spirit and in the realm of human experience" (Lüthi 1982, pp. 8-9). Or, legends are about emotion and folktales are about action.

This emotional "one-dimensionality," as Lüthi calls it, is one of the biggest changes in attitude toward witches between the seventeenth and nineteenth centuries. In the age of the witch hunts, witches were figures of legend, those amazingly evil beings who cannot be explained but only narrated. By the nineteenth century, they are merely the motivating factors behind the hero's actions. This is astonishing, given that in the throes of a witch mania the one thing that can be said with assurance to have been real about the whole thing was that people's emotions were aroused to a frenzy by the very thought of witches. Even if they were projecting their own fears and anxieties onto the most vulnerable members of society and then purging them through torture and execution, the emotions were real.

It is interesting that the effect of a witch in a folktale is generally to stop action: witches and their ilk above all are jailers, keeping Hansel in his fattening-cell, Rapunzel in her tower, Snow White seemingly dead in her glass coffin, Sleeping Beauty, appropriately enough, asleep. These are not witches who ride on their broomsticks impossible distances to dance with the Devil; they are witches who stay put and draw their victims in. Real-world witch beliefs were based in the fear that witches, by stealing everything fruitful and growing (from crops to children to men's penises), would cause individuals to live in a kind of wasteland. In folktales, this theft of fertility has been metaphorized into causing a kind of enforced stasis in which the hero or heroine might physically grow—Hansel gets fatter, Rapunzel's hair grows from her tower to the ground—but movement is prohibited. Nonetheless, the folktale witch is metaphorical rather than real. Rather than harkening back to Medea, she is more like Medusa, turning everything to immobile stone.

At the turn of the twentieth century, L. Frank Baum published the first of his many books about the land of Oz, *The Wizard of Oz* (1900), and introduced two of the iconic witches of the twentieth century, the Wicked Witch of the West and Glinda the Good, as well as a male magician, the Wizard himself. Baum deliberately created a fairytale world with the type of one-dimensionality that Lüthi comments upon: talking animals, flying monkeys, magic slippers, animated scarecrows and tin men, all a normal state of affairs but all in a locale far, far from a gray and mundane home.

However, Baum also deliberately created a world in which there were none of the "terrors" of authentic folktales because he felt that children should be shielded from anxiety-arousing elements in literature. (Baum suffered from a weak heart and tried to organize his own life to avoid as much stress, anxiety, and sudden shock as possible.) In fact, at one point in *The Land of Oz* (1904), the sequel to *The Wizard of Oz*, Glinda threatens to kill the witch Mombi unless she confesses what she has done with the missing heir to the throne of Oz, and the soft-hearted Tinman protests that "It would be an awful thing to kill anyone—even old Mombi!" Glinda replies, "But it is merely a threat … I will not put Mombi to death, because she will prefer to tell me the truth" (Baum 1904, p. 261). The thing is, Mombi is standing right there in front of them, so Glinda has effectively detoothed her threat in the interests of allaying the childish anxieties of Baum's audience; Mombi nonetheless immediately capitulates.

Even so, Baum's primary villains throughout his Oz series are witches. The evil magic of witchcraft is contrasted with the benevolent magic of "sorceresses" and the fraudulent magic of (male) wizards. Baum initially introduces the land of Oz as ruled by four "witches," with good witches in the north and south and wicked witches in the east and west, with the Wizard ruling over all of them from the center, the Emerald City. (This division, oddly enough, echoes the medieval Irish concept of the island of Ireland composed of four quarters—which, although they were technically focused in the northeast, northwest, southeast, and southwest, were conceived as north, south, east, and west—ruled by kings, and a high king over all of them at Tara, the ritual center of the emerald isle.) Dorothy kills the Wicked Witches by accident, crushing one with her cyclone-launched house and melting the other with a bucket of water, and she is assisted on her entrance to Oz by the good Witch of the North, who looks like a very old lady, and on her exit by Glinda the Good, the Witch of the South, who uses her magic to remain eternally young.

When Dorothy first meets the Witch of the North, she is confused by the concept of a "good witch" because she has been told by Aunt Em that a) all witches are wicked, and b) all witches are dead and have been for a long time. The Witch of the North explains that she, personally, knows that some witches are good, because she herself is a good witch, and conjectures that the reason all the witches are dead in the exotic kingdom of Kansas must be that Kansas is a civilized country, and witches, wizards, sorceresses, and magicians cannot live in civilized countries. Oz, however, is not now and never has been civilized, and furthermore is cut off from the rest of the world by an impassible desert, and so witches and wizards still live there.

The magic of Oz is a mixed bag. The Witch of the North can transport herself from place to place in the blink of an eye, and she has a magic scroll that reveals the correct action to take in a particular circumstance. The powers of the Witch of the East are unspecified, but they were stronger than those of the Witch of the North, otherwise the latter would have overthrown the former and set the Munchkins free from her wicked dominion. The Witch of the West is also tyrannical over her people, the Winkies, and she can command a variety of threatening animals: wolves, crows, bees, and flying monkeys. Glinda's magic primarily resides in her wisdom. She is the *dea ex machina* who provides the solution to the problem no one else can solve, usually by revealing the magical properties of something that's been there all along (like Dorothy's silver slippers) or providing some other form of magical transport, like a magic carpet in *Ozma of Oz* (1907) that makes it possible to traverse the desert that surrounds Oz. Indeed, for a witch who rarely leaves her own quadrant of Oz, she is especially apt to provide transportation solutions.

In *The Land of Oz*, the Scarecrow states the philosophy of magic: "All magic is unnatural, and for that reason is to be feared and avoided" (Baum 1904, p. 161). However, the difference between good magic and bad magic, in the Oz magical economy, is that good magic is used by rulers to benefit their subjects, while bad magic is used to gain and maintain political power. The Wizard's magic is ambiguous because his use of it has been both "good" and "bad." He used his magic to wrest the throne of Oz from King Pastoria, Ozma's father, and he uses magic tricks to retain his power, but he is otherwise a benevolent ruler of his people. He can provide "magical" solutions for psychological blocks such as afflict the Scarecrow, Woodman, and Lion, who are intelligent, loving, and brave but don't realize it, but his attempts to solve a real-world problem such as getting Dorothy back to Kansas fail. Even though he comes up with a workable means of transportation that gets *him* out of Oz, ultimately it does not help Dorothy.

The Wizard comes across as a pathetic fraud in *The Wizard of Oz*, a showman who uses stage tricks to pass himself off as something he isn't, but in *The Land of Oz* it appears that he does have some magical powers because he makes a deal with Mombi to teach her magic in return for her hiding the rightful heir to the throne, Ozma. Mombi's designation varies: initially, she is said not to be a witch because she lives in the Land of the Gillikins under the dominion of the Witch of the North, and since sthe latter is a good witch, she has decreed that no other witch may live in her dominions. Therefore, Mombi claims to be nothing more than a sorceress, or at most a wizardess. This suggests a hierarchy of magic in Oz, with witches the most powerful and sorcerers the least, which casts an interesting light on the status of the "wizard." (In *Dorothy and the Wizard in Oz* [1908], the Wizard states that one wizard is the equivalent of three sorcerers.) Yet when the band of heroes finally goes to Glinda to solve their problem, she is called a "queen" and a "sorceress" rather than a "witch" as she had been in the first book; *Glinda of Oz* (1920), the last book of the series written by Baum (for the series continued under five more writers after his death), opens by identifying her as "the good Sorceress of Oz" and Oz itself as a "Fairyland" (Baum 1920, p. 13). The original distinction between "good witches" and "wicked witches" is too fine for Baum to sustain, so he reverts to using "witch" for old, ugly women who use magic greedily to obtain illicit power, while beautiful, young women who use magic wisely for the benefit of others are "sorceresses." Ozma, furthermore, is often described as a fairy, and in *The Magic of Oz* (1919) it is explained that the reason why no one ever dies in Oz is precisely because of this fairy quality to the land and its ruler.

The Wizard's morality is rehabilitated and Mombi's darkened in *Dorothy and the Wizard in Oz*, when the Wizard returns to Oz for good and is made Ozma's official court wizard. This time, the story is that Oz formerly had one ruler, always named Oz if male, Ozma if female. Mombi had managed to kidnap and imprison Ozma's grandfather and the rule of the country divided among herself and three other wicked witches. Two of those witches were overthrown in turn by the good Witch of the North and Glinda in the south (note that Glinda is not designated a witch); the Wizard, the initials of whose given name spelled O.Z. P.I.N.H.E.A.D. and therefore he only used his first two initials, landed in his balloon and was taken for the rightful ruler. He used tricks to intimidate the witches and built the Emerald City for himself. His magic is therefore "humbug": as Dorothy notes, "He can do several wonderful things—if he knows how. But he can't wiz a single thing if he hasn't the tools and machinery to work with" (Baum 1908, p. 149). This implies that humbug magic depends on science (especially engineering) while "real" magic is somehow natural and innate.

The constant changes in attitude toward and nomenclature of magic and its practitioners shows that Baum was not working from a deliberate and well-thought-out philosophy of magic but merely picking up whatever was available in popular conceptions of magic and witchcraft and useful at the moment. The plots of Oz books usually involve travel to new areas of the country where odd and unique individuals reside, and then a return to the Emerald City. There is rarely much conflict because, fairytale-like, there is always a magical tool to save the day at the crucial moment. As a result, most of the energy of the narrative goes toward describing the magical wonders of Oz, all of which are beautiful, luxurious, and rationally efficient.

There are three general types of inhabitants at Ozma's court. One group comprises Americans who have found their way to Oz through various cataclysms—Dorothy's first three visits are occasioned by being caught in a cyclone, being washed overboard at sea in a dreadful storm, and being swallowed in a crack in the ground during a horrific earthquake (that one occurred a mere two years after the San Francisco quake of 1906, so Baum was obviously reacting to topical disasters). Another group comprises individuals made of inanimate substances that have been magically brought to life, such as the Scarecrow, Tinman, Patchwork Girl, Jack Pumpkinhead, and so on. Finally there are the talking animals, such as the Cowardly Lion, Hungry Tiger, Eureka the Pink Kitten, Hank the Mule, and Billina the Yellow Hen. These latter two categories represent the effects of magic rather than the performance of magic itself. Ozma, Glinda, and the Wizard are the only people allowed to practice magic within the boundaries of Oz. Glinda's magic exhibits her wisdom, the Wizard's his ingenuity, which conforms to the stereotypically female and male gender roles that inform Baum's work.

Ozma is a somewhat different case. The story that relates how she comes to regain her throne illustrates several possibilities for rule, each associated in different ways with magic and with gender, none of which turns out to be satisfactory. The rightful rule of Oz had not been gender-specific, falling to whatever heir happened to be available. (The absence of death in Oz is ignored in this formulation.) Then the incumbent king is overthrown by wicked witches, who have used magic to become tyrants. Two of them are, in turn, overthrown by good witches, who rule benevolently but do not have the power to take the entire country. The Wizard arrives and manages to trick his way into power, but he cannot maintain his humbug forever. He is succeeded by the Scarecrow at the center, while the Tinman replaces the Witch of the West. Now all of Oz is under benevolent power, but both the Scarecrow and Tinman are depicted, at this point, as being somewhat ineffective if well-meaning rulers—the Scarecrow is not as smart as he thinks, and the Woodman seems to care more about his appearance than anything else. The Scarecrow is overthrown in turn by General Jinjur and her army of girls, who rebel apparently for lack of anything better to do. Rule by males who practice good magic, males who are the subject of magic, wickedly magical females, nonmagical females, and even "sorceresses" are all insufficient to bring all of Oz under good rule. The answer turns out to be Ozma who, although she is born female, had been turned by Mombi into the boy Tip for the better part of her life before being restored to his true form. Ozma thus unites both male and female, magic and nonmagic, and transcends them all as an ageless fairy. (Stop giggling.)

In the eighteenth and early nineteenth centuries, magic and witchcraft were still regarded as dangerous topics and literary works that used ideas about the supernatural were decidedly adult fare, whether the topic at hand was concerned with sex, such as *The Monk*, or free will, such as *Faust*. By the end of the nineteenth century, however, magic had become a topic for children's stories, whether oral or literary. In an era when machines and electricity were transforming the lives of Europeans and Americans at an unprecedented rate, the supernatural was old-fashioned. The real "magic" lay in technology. The distinction between intellectual, scientific magic performed by males and instinctual, natural magic performed by females, which had first emerged in the Middle Ages, gained additional levels of meaning: female magic was fusty, folksy, and irrational, while male magic became increasingly indistinguishable from science. Male magic affected the physical world, while female magic affected the emotional world.

As L. Frank Baum's health declined, he moved to Hollywood, California, for the weather. As a young man he had been an actor, playwright, and the manager of a theater company, and it was not surprising that in California he should become interested in the new technology of film. In 1914 he formed the Oz Film Manufacturing Company and made several silent movies based on his novels. In *His Majesty, the Scarecrow of Oz* (1914), the plot revolves around Mombi's scheme to remove the heart of Princess Gloria so that she will marry the man chosen for her by her father, King Krewl, rather than loving the gardener boy Pon. The film uses all the tricks of early silent film as people are transformed in shape, size, and species, but the narrative is a purely traditional one—ugly old ladies messing around with love spells.

Although the Oz books were enormously popular in their time, it is questionable whether they would have retained their status in the changing cultural climate of the later twentieth century on their own. The Grimms began to tone down the violence, cruelty, and sexuality in their collection of oral tales as soon as they realized that the tales had come to be regarded as children's fare. Baum deliberately set out to create a fairy world that eliminated even the little violence that remained after three-quarters of a century of bowdlerization of folktales, as children became ever more tightly wrapped in cotton wool to preserve their pristine innocence. Yet *The Wizard of Oz* was published in the same year as Sigmund Freud's *Interpretation of Dreams*, and the rise of Freudian psychology spelled doom to the idea of children as asexual angels. Violence and sexuality came to be seen underlying every human act and the appearance of innocence was taken merely to indicate powerful repression.

For most people born in the twentieth century, the iconic image of Oz comes not from the books but from the 1939 movie, and of all the changes the movie made in its source material, perhaps the most significant is the depiction of the Wicked Witch of the West, the subject of nightmares for generations. Baum's books and movies were confections more akin to the masques of early modern royal courts, in which the story was merely an excuse for everyone to dress up and to be wowed by court technicians' state-of-the-art pyrotechnics. The actress Margaret Hamilton gave the Wicked Witch her teeth again, and with real, if cinematic, threats of torture and death, magic was once more something to worry about.

CHAPTER 9

FROM MYTH TO RELIGION

FROM THE EARLIEST TIMES, it was believed that witches were apt to worship certain goddesses, Hecate chief among them, who provided them with their knowledge and their power. However, the idea that every worshiper of a particular deity was a witch did not arise until that deity was named as Satan, and as has been seen, the concept of an organized religion devoted to evil works and Devil worship was a paranoid fantasy of Christians rather than an authentic folk practice. Evil works have tended to be more disorganized than not throughout human history, which is why the organized ones (the Holocaust springs to mind) are so remarkable. Throughout the nineteenth century the practice of ritual magic took on many of the trappings of religion, but it was not until the twentieth century that witchcraft, or as it came to call itself, Wicca, could be said to have become a religion that practiced magic rather than a magic with religious aspirations.

In the late antique and early medieval periods, the primary religious dichotomy in Europe was between paganism and Christianity. In the High Middle Ages it was between Christianity and Islam in the arena of the Crusades and between orthodox Christianity and assorted heresies closer to home. The early modern period was divided between Catholicism and Protestantism. By the Industrial era, however, the philosophical tension between science and religion took center stage. Science provided practical answers to questions that religion addressed in metaphorical terms, and promised to answer questions that religion wouldn't touch with anything other than faith. It began to seem that the strength of religion lay in its ability to create and support community rather than its ability to provide answers to metaphysical questions. Mainstream religion was increasingly associated with the provision of a moral code and a set of proscriptions upon behavior; spiritual sustenance was more and more often sought in the exotic, whether that was Catholicism for a Methodist, Buddhism for a Catholic, or theosophy for a Jew.

Just as science had driven a wedge between theology and the physical world, the spiritualist movement had lessened religion's dominion over the afterlife. Spiritualism was on the decline at the end of the nineteenth century, but the carnage of World War I breathed life back into the movement. Partly it was to make contact with loved ones lost on the battlefield in uncertain circumstances—many of the major battles of the war were so bloody and lasted so long that it was impossible to recover bodies and ship them home for burial. The influenza epidemic that swept through the world in 1918 brought another tidal wave of unexpected death. Between war and the flu, the second decade of the twentieth century saw an unprecedented number of deaths that left the survivors without closure, as their descendants at the end of the century would put it. Seances, whether fraudulent or not, offered that closure.

In addition to providing exciting technological advances that made life easier and more fun, such as electricity, telephones, and cinema, science was providing new kinds of insight into the past. Digging up the physical remains of the past had been a hobby of gentlemen and grave-robbers for quite some time, but it was only with the end of the nineteenth century that the scientific discipline of archaeology began to coalesce, with the aim of understanding how people of the past had lived, rather than merely accumulating pretty treasures. Since ancient civilizations usually put a large portion of their time, energy, and resources into religious sites—temples, sanctuaries, statues of gods, ritual accouterments—early twentieth century archaeology was revealing the flip side of the religions demonized by Christianity, whether the paganisms of the Middle East from the Old Testament or those of ancient Europe denounced by early Church Fathers. Hand in hand with the study of folklore in the nineteenth century had come the rise of historical linguistics, and people were now interested in and capable of reading what texts remained of these pre-Christian and pre-Jewish peoples. Even when the texts had only been written under Christian supervision, as in Ireland, the radical difference between the native traditions they captured and the mental world preserved in Greek and Latin provided yet another vantage point from which to understand spirituality. For those who retained their commitment to mainstream Christianity and Judaism, archaeology offered the promise of proving that the "myths" of the Bible were, in fact, true.

Onto this stage, on which the metaphysical was physical and there was a rational explanation for everything, walked Margaret Alice Murray. Although Murray's official area of expertise was Egyptology (she trained as a linguist and became a specialist in Egyptian hieroglyphics, working on Sir Flinders Petrie's excavations of Abydos in Egypt in the 1890s), during World War I, when she was unable to travel to Egypt due to the hostilities, she turned her attention to the witch trials of the early modern era, especially Scotland. Murray was strongly influenced by the anthropological theories of Sir James George Frazer concerning the evolution of man and religion and, in particular, his theory of the divine king, who must be ritually sacrificed in order to preserve the fertility of the land and the balance of the cosmos.

She was also a member of the Folklore Society, where she was exposed to the ideas, work, and controversies of influential folklorists such as Lawrence Gomme and Andrew Lang. Folklorists at that time were very much of the opinion that the quaint and harmless folklore of the present was a faded survival of archaic and often savage religion and mythology. Murray combed the records of the witch trials with an eye toward uncovering a primitive religion still being practiced under the guise of folklore. And she found it.

The Witch Cult in Western Europe (1921) was Murray's first monograph on the subject, although she had been publishing articles and presenting papers advancing her thesis since her interest was first aroused in 1915. Murray proposed that the Satanic witch cult persecuted by the Church was, in fact, a pagan fertility cult that had persisted in secret since the Christianization of Europe. The "Devil" worshiped by witches was in fact the Horned God, known in the classical world as Pan but called by Murray Dianus (the male version of the goddess Diana, so closely associated with witchcraft throughout the medieval period).

Murray identified two forms of witchcraft. The first she called "operative witchcraft," by which she meant the charms and spells of folk magic practiced throughout the world. What she termed "Dianic" or "ritual witchcraft" was, she claimed, an organized religion dating to pre-Christian times; indeed, she felt that the nature of the rituals suggested a pre-agricultural origin and she is the first to have adopted the Paleolithic cave drawing of a man apparently dancing in a stag costume from the Caverne des Trois Freres in Ariege, France, as the archetypal image of a shamanic pagan priest (Murray 1931, fig. 1). Taking a hint from Cotton Mather, the seventeenth century Massachusetts Puritan who stated that witches were organized like Congregationalists, Murray declared that the Dianic religion consisted of a "coven" of elders who managed local affairs and one man who served as the chief mediator between the people and the deity (Murray 1931, p. 65).

It was this latter personage whom Murray believed was the "Devil" who was said to have sexual intercourse with witches in their debauched revels. This man wore an outfit that included a peculiar head-dress that led to him being described as horned. In fact, the pervasive description of the Devil as having cold flesh, particularly a cold penis, led Murray to posit that the leader of the coven was dressed in an all-over costume of leather. The religion, as Murray reconstructed it from records of witch trials, required its adherents to be "introduced" (a ritual Murray compared to the sponsorship role of Christian godparents), then renounce their allegiance to Christianity and make new vows to the witch deity, including signing a covenant with the "Devil." The initiate might then be (re)baptized in their new faith, sometimes acquiring a witch's mark that Murray suggests was a tattoo. The normal assemblies of the religion consisted of Sabbaths, a general meeting of the whole congregation, and what she called Esbats, which were business gatherings by a smaller group—the business being the practice of magic for the benefit of clients or to harm opponents. Sabbaths also included an opportunity for members to discuss their magical practices and ask advice of the Master. Both Sabbaths and Esbats ended with feasting and dancing. Murray claimed that witches practiced four forms of sacrifice: of the witch's own blood, of an animal, of a human being (often a child), and of the god himself. The types of magic that witches practiced, according to Murray, particularly focused on fertility (both promoting it and blocking it) and rain-making.

The aspect of Murray's hypothesis that raised the most academic eyebrows was her claim that Britain had been only superficially converted to Christianity, taking on a veneer of that religion in order to maintain social respectability but in truth continuing to practice the Old Religion in secret. Initially she made a distinction between the folk, witch religion of the rural peasant classes versus the Christianity of the upper classes; by her third book, *The Divine King in England* (1954), she was claiming that the monarchs of Britain were hard-core pagan witches who submitted to periodic human sacrifice for the good of the nation.

This theory derives from Murray's scholarly allegiance to Frazer's theory, as expounded in *The Golden Bough* (1890-1905), of the divine king, who was periodically sacrificed to secure the fertility of the land and its people. Frazer suggested that over time, in order to retain competent rulers, the practice arose of naming a substitute who was killed in the king's place. Thus, Murray claimed that William Rufus (d. 1100), who died in a suspicious hunting accident, was actually a ritual sacrifice as king, while Thomas à Becket (1118-1170), sacrilegiously murdered in Canturbury Cathedral, was a substitute sacrifice, as were Joan of Arc (d. 1431) and Gilles de Rais (1404-1440). Although Murray's more extreme claims are hard to swallow, she was operating from the reasonably defensible position that people are usually reluctant to change habits that are believed to ensure health, fertility, and luck, and are more apt to adopt a new religion in addition to, rather than instead of, the old one.

Murray claimed to be merely describing the practice of the religion as she found it in the records, but from the beginning other scholars protested that, while she did not make up any of her data, she was guilty of ignoring data in the records that did not support her hypothesis. Much of her description of the kind of magic that witches practiced raises the question of just where she saw the dividing line between "operative" and "ritual" witchcraft—rain-making, effecting fertility, charms and spells are all concerns and techniques of folk magic. The real difference for Murray, it seems, was that ritual witchcraft was organized, with a hierarchical structure that was consistent across Western Europe even though there was no central authority, such as a papacy, to maintain its consistency. This is the part of her thesis that is least supported by her data. However, Murray's thesis was, for a while, popularly accepted and helped to consolidate the believe in the secret survival of paganism. Murray's focus on Scottish witch trials also reinforced the association of "paganism" with Celtic religion and mythology.

An indirect influence on the intellectual evolution of Wicca was Robert Graves's *The White Goddess* (1948). Although Graves was writing a myth about poetic composition, he located it in an explicitly pagan context, drawing together Greek and Welsh myth to create a purely European goddess who was represented by the moon and its phases. Balanced with the goddess was her divine son—she was successively his mother, wife, and widow. This pairing actually has roots in the Middle East more than in Greece or Wales (or much of anywhere else in Europe); it is the pairing of Inanna and Dumuzi, Ishtar and Tammuz, Cybele and Attis. For Graves, "true poetry" derives from the worship of this goddess in her cyclical aspects.

The true centerpiece of *The White Goddess*, however, is Graves's analysis of the poem *Cad Goddeu* ("The Battle of the Trees"), attributed to the legendary sixth century poet Taliesin and found in the fourteenth century Book of Taliesin. This long and obscure poem appears to be about a battle among a variety of trees and shrubs; its references are enigmatic at best and untranslatable at worst: "...ivy for its beauty; sea gorse for terror;/Cherries mocked; birch for high-mindedness..." (Ford 1977, p. 185). Graves claimed that the key to understanding the poem was to be found in the Irish ogham alphabet, which we have already met in connection with the warrior-scribe Cennfaeladh. The names of the ogham letters, in what appears to have been the most standard form, were the names of trees, and Graves held that the puzzling characteristics ascribed to the trees in *Cad Goddeu* referred to arcane, mystical, and poetic worship of the White Goddess.

Graves's work has never been taken seriously by academic Celticists (although he does occasionally make an enlightening hit), in particular because he was working from a rather bad translation of the poem and so his mystical correspondences are not only far-fetched but, when reading other translations, completely nonexistent. His myth of the goddess and her son, however, refined the theme of the divine king sacrificed at ritual intervals, which formed the core of Frazer's work but tended to get lost in tangential undergrowth as *The Golden Bough* expanded to a dozen volumes. Graves's interpretation of the myth focused on the goddess, however, rather than the sacrificed king/son. His poetic mythology was matriarchal to the core. He also provided an introduction to Welsh mythology in the pages of his work, a mythology which, up to that point, had been very much the concern of specialists and the Welsh alone. Although there were several fairytale-like translations and retellings published for children in the early part of the twentieth century, Graves was the first to provide an analysis of the tales for a popular audience. *The White Goddess* did much to make Celtic, especially Welsh, mythology the pagan source par excellence.

Returning to the Folklore Society, one of Margaret Murray's colleagues there was a retired tea grower and civil servant named Gerald Gardner who had spent much of his life in the Far East—Sri Lanka, Borneo, Malaysia. He had been interested in archaeology, native religions, spiritualism, and nudism during the years of his working life, and when he retired to England, he devoted himself to occult interests full time. While Murray claimed to have discovered evidence that witchcraft was a real religion practiced in the past, Gardner claimed to be practicing that religion in the present. He said that he was inducted into a coven of hereditary witches located in the New Forest in 1939, and as he learned more about their practices, he wanted to write a book about witchcraft to correct the many misapprehensions about them in the popular culture. His high priestess initially forbade any writing about witchcraft, but eventually the coven agreed he might write in the guise of fiction. This became *High Magic's Aid* (1949). Two years later, the anti-witchcraft laws of 1736 were repealed; this meant that not only was witchcraft now deemed irrational, but that to say one was a witch was no longer even considered fraud. This removed one of the main obstacles to Gardner writing about his experiences as a witch in nonfictional form. In 1954, he published *Witchcraft Today*.

Like Murray, Gardner claimed that his religion was the same-old same-old (or same-Old) practiced under Christian noses since the time of (ostensible) conversion. Later scholars, however, have noted that Gardner's witchcraft forwarded many of his non-magical interests, especially the practice of performing rituals in the nude, or "sky clad." The use of a knife as a ritual instrument recalled Gardner's earliest publication, a book on the Malaysian *kris*. Gardner's witchcraft consisted of three degrees of training, each of which ideally took a year and a day to learn.

Rituals were highly formalized and, in contrast to Murray's female-friendly but male-led witchcraft theory, were performed by a high priestess with a priest as a secondary officiant. The power of the priestess, however, was merely ceded to her by the priest, which somewhat undercuts the notion of female autonomy. While Murray posited a male deity, the Horned God, as the focus of witch worship, Gardner's witchcraft worshiped a goddess mated with a god (literally—the reenactment of this sexual union by the high priestess and her high priest was called the Great Rite). Gardner's witchcraft, which has come to be known as Gardnerian Wicca, is highly organized, with hierarchies of power and lineages of covens carefully tracked. It is much more concerned with doing what is "right" than with doing "what works," as many other Wiccan traditions have evolved to believe.

One of Gardner's chief rituals was achieving magical ends through the raising of a "cone of power," the accumulated psychic energy aroused through dancing in a circle, outdoors, naked. Walls and clothes, he said, inhibited the movement of the energy and the ability to focus it where the coven wanted it to go. Gardner also insisted on a balance of male and female energy in rituals. As the whole notion of a dance-induced cone of power suggests, Gardner's magic was accomplished in a state of ecstasy and trance—a kind of group shamanism. Balancing this experiential, ecstatic element of magic was the Book of Shadows, the textual source of Gardnerian ritual. This collection of instructions and invocations had to be hand-copied by each initiate into the coven. It thus became the literary equivalent of an orally transmitted tradition. Gardner's Book of Shadows, as scholars including Aidan Kelly and Ronald Hutton have shown, had its roots in diverse magical texts and traditions, including Freemasonry, Rosicrucianism, Aleister Crowley's Thelemic magical tradition, and Kabbalah, as well as rites with no traceable provenance that may be authentic hereditary traditions or which may have been of Gardner's own devising.

Hutton describes the tension between syncretism and innovation in Gardner's Wiccan rituals thus:

> Like Masonry and Co-Masonry, the ceremonies taught knowledge and skill through three progressive degrees of initiation, and included "working tools." Like Co-Masonry and the Golden Dawn, they involved women members on an equal basis, and like the Golden Dawn they operated practical magic; the seasonal rites always left space for ad hoc magical workings. Like the Golden Dawn also, they attempted to draw divinity into, or from, human beings. Unlike all of these, they were conducted by groups led by a high priestess and a high priest, whose relationship mirrored that of the two deities. Freemasonry ... shunned the north as the place of darkness; Gardner's ceremonies not only recognized the north as a place of divinity and elemental power ... but treated it as the quarter of greatest sanctity. By forcing its members to recognize the merit in the dark, as in its feminism, its unqualified paganism, its counter-cultural deities, and its insistence upon complete nudity during its rites, it was challenging a whole series of norms in the most dramatic way.... Like all the magical or quasi-magical societies which had flourished since the seventeenth century, this one concealed innovation under a language of continuity or restitution; except that it went one better than the lot, claiming to descend from the paleolithic in the manner suggested by Margaret Murray (Hutton 1999, p. 236).

The phrase "new tradition" is an oxymoron, and as Hutton notes, new religions bolster their authority by claiming to be old ones, often under the guise of returning to the original truths from which the contemporary religion has strayed (the tactic taken by early Protestantism) or by claiming to complete the previous religion (as Christianity claims to complete Judaism). Gardner's claim to have been initiated into an archaic religion dating back to the very beginnings of human existence appears to have been just such an authoritative claim. It ironically ended up by arousing enormous controversy over the truth of the claim. By and large, the possibility of a religion lasting that long and in secret is untenable. However, just because the largest parameter of the claim is impossible does not necessarily prove the opposite, that Gardner made up Wicca out of whole cloth. Hutton's research shows that Gardner's religion evolved out of many threads in Western European, and especially Anglo-American, culture. The coven into which he was initiated was probably not practicing authentic folk magic but was rather an offshoot of the many proto-pagan magical organizations of the late nineteenth and early twentieth centuries.

The fact that Gardnerian witches have had a tendency to claim that their magic is the only authentic tradition has also thrown into doubt the claims of other traditions to authenticity. Many of the people who claim to be "hereditary witches" may well have had ancestors who were local cunning folk and who passed down their knowledge through the family. However, most of these people did not belong to the kind of highly organized and hierarchical tradition that Gardner established. Groups such as the Friulian *benandanti*, Rumanian *Calusari*, Lapp shamans, and all those who "followed Diana" in various forms also have descendants living today who may authentically claim "witchcraft" in their blood. Then there are the descendants of those falsely accused of witchcraft during the witch hunts—including that modern magician Walt Disney, a direct descendant of George Burroughs, executed at Salem.

The biggest proliferation of modern witches has been prospective rather than retrospective, however. Parallel to Gardner's Wicca were Aleister Crowley's Thelemic orders, the source of the dictum "Do as thou wilt shall be the whole of the Law." The focus on Will, which is based in the human rather than located in a deity, made Crowley's mysticism more philosophical than religious. Alex Sanders founded the Alexandrian tradition of Wicca (the name is actually not in reference to his first name, but to the Hellenistic city of Alexandria in Egypt, a focal point of Late Antique Hermeticism) in the 1960s; this was largely based on Gardnerian Wicca with nudity optional, different names for deities, different uses of working tools, and rather more emphasis on ritual magic instead of ecstatic power-raising. Faery Wicca was formulated by Victor H. Anderson and contains a strongly shamanic element and also a unique blending of Hawaiian and Welsh supernatural belief underpinning it. The feminist movement of the 1970s led to perhaps the most important innovation in Wicca— Dianic witchcraft, a highly eclectic practice that focuses almost exclusively on the Goddess and, in contrast to the very organized and lineage-bound Gardnerian tradition, is extremely improvisational.

Interest in the feminine divine has largely focused on pagan goddesses, although there is a growing Christian feminist movement aimed at restoring the feminine aspects of divinity that have been suppressed in patriarchal religion. Goddess spirituality had its earliest roots in Wicca, modifying Gardnerian Wicca by downplaying or downright eliminating the Horned God in favor of the Goddess.

In the 1970s, the concept of the Goddess was undergoing a significant change. Archaeologist Marija Gimbutas's *Goddesses and Gods of Old Europe, 6500-3500 BC* (1974) presented the picture of a matriarchal age of peace and egalitarianism under the patronage of a goddess with different local names but universal quality. Monica Sjoo and Barbara Mor's *The Great Cosmic Mother* (1981) traced the worship of the Goddess from the Neolithic to the early Bronze Age, when her multivalence became narrowed to simply mother goddess. Merlin Stone's *When God Was a Woman* (1976) uncovered the suppressed history of goddess worship in the Near East during Biblical times, suggesting that the patriarchal format of Judeo-Christian religion was retrospectively invented by the writers of the Old and New Testaments in order to bolster their claim to religious and cultural authority.

Gardnerian Wicca, with its British roots, spoke of a goddess of the natural, physical world who would be, technically, universal, since the natural world encompasses the whole globe, but who was conceptualized in practical terms as the goddess of the nature right around here, which happened to be England. Gardnerian Wicca looks to the Celts for its archaic roots, as does Faery Wicca. (Among the ethnicities of Great Britain, the Celts have always been the archetypal Other, the "them" contrasted with the Anglo-Saxon "us.") In the 1970s, the Goddess became both more universal and more specific. She was conceived as the Great Mother of All, the original form of all human religion, and every culture gave her a local habitation and a name. Women could focus their attention on whichever form of the Goddess spoke most to them, whether Kali or Cerridwen or Diana or Isis, while understanding that all these goddesses, in all their variety, were manifestations of the single, universal Goddess.

On one hand, this universal goddess harkens back to the Isis of *The Golden Ass*, who claims that all nations have their own names for her but her true name is Isis; on the other hand, there is a tendency to gloss over the differences between goddesses and between cultures, to focus on the lowest common divine denominator, a trend that derived from Theosophy and its Ascended Masters lurking behind every world religion. The aspects of a goddess that may reflect an individual culture's ideas about the female and the divine are dismissed as late, patriarchal revisions intended to diminish the Goddess. There can also be a tendency to regard the Goddess as wholly beneficent and anything dark or dangerous associated with the female divine as patriarchal denigration. While many worshipers came in the late twentieth century to accept a more rounded, nuanced vision of the Goddess, in the 1970s and early 1980s the polarities of male and female, divine and degraded established by mainstream Christianity and Judaism were simply reversed.

One of the most influential thinkers in the Goddess spirituality movement is Starhawk, author of *The Spiral Dance* (1979). Unlike the purely female covens worshiping only goddesses of Dianic witchcraft, Starhawk's theology is aimed at healing the hostilities between men and women by proposing a different model of power—rather than "power over," her paganism seeks to have "power with" or "power within," emphasizing egalitarianism and self-sufficiency and control rather than hierarchy based in gender, class, or ethnicity. In an interview, Starhawk described her inspiration for writing *The Spiral Dance* as based in her feminism, but also in an understanding that the entire cosmos is alive:

I ... felt it was important for women to have other models of spirituality besides the patriarchal ones. Also, it seemed important to have models of spirituality that were earth-based and earth-centered. There's nothing in the book that's revealing secrets that shouldn't be revealed—I've never been a great one to shout "Oh, this is so secret! This is so secret!" That really tends to support a kind of self-inflation. The real secrets of the Craft are secrets that can't be *told* ... because you have to *experience* them (Vale and Sulak 2001, p. 7).

The Spiral Dance concludes with a chapter titled "Creating Religion: Toward the Future" in which Starhawk calls for paganism to become a collective force to change the world for the better. Throughout the book, she emphasizes that the rituals and spells she outlines are suggestions based on what has worked in the past, but also encourages her readers, whether working alone or in groups, to follow their intuition in creating rituals that feel right to them. The accumulation of "power within" is the surest guide to "what works."

It has been noted by many observers both inside and outside the pagan community that Gardnerian Wicca, with its secrecy, ranks of initiation, and insistence on conformity to tradition reflects a more general British interest in hierarchy and tradition, while American witchcrafts, Dianic or otherwise, emphasize novelty, individualism, and freedom of choice in a way that is, in contrast, very American. In a similar way, British people visiting the United States are often appalled by the number of ways in which they must designate how they want their sandwiches prepared in a restaurant, while Americans in Britain become outraged when their sandwich comes with mayonnaise on it whether they like it or not. Just as every generation gets the Stonehenge it deserves (as Jacquetta Hawkes famously stated), every generation, and every nationality, gets the witches it deserves, too.

Although Wicca was the wellspring of Goddess spirituality, over the ensuing three decades a distinction has arisen between worship and magic. There are many Pagans who only worship the Goddess, without attempting to influence the material world thereby except by their natural actions, while there are many who practice magic as an attempt to use the supernatural to cause changes in the natural world according to their will, without necessarily regarding the spirits who assist them as deities. Then there are those who worship the Goddess, or the Goddess and God together, and practice magic as a means of manifesting the Goddess's peace, bounty, and healing in the physical world.

Where there was only Gardnerian Wicca as a pagan alternative to mainstream religion in the 1950s, within fifty years there are so many varieties of Wicca that it is impossible to make any general statement about the religion without pages of qualification. The situation is even further complicated by the rise of "solitaries," witches who practice magic or simply worship the Goddess alone, without working in a coven or other organized group. Some solitaries practice alone most of the time, but join others for special rituals on occasion. In the United States, summer camp gatherings have arisen as opportunities for Wiccans and other Pagans of all stripes to come together in a kind of nonecumenical Paganism to celebrate (often the summer solstice), network, and share information and ideas, then disperse to practice their own traditions in groups or alone for the rest of the year. The more solitary a witch is, the more likely he or she is to practice on the basis of "what works."

When early Christians dismissed their religious opponents as pagans, one meaning they intended to convey was that the religion of "pagans" was empty ritual—only Christianity had access to the true God who made ritual meaningful and effective. Likewise, when early Protestants accused Catholics as being no better than pagans, they too were referring to a perceived emptiness of ritual. Christianity in general has swung between extremes of formal structure mediated by priests and informal, direct contact with the Holy Spirit. Those offshoots that are the most enthusiastic (in the literal sense of "filled with god,") are invariably regarded with suspicion by more sedate and mainstream sects until they, too, tone down their excesses.

Thus the Methodists, Quakers, and Shakers in their early years were renowned for a kind of madness that overtook their adherents as they bypassed the formal structure of the Anglican Church and made direct contact with God—it was their excesses that lead to the nicknames of "quaker" and "shaker" to describe the trembling and near hysteria of their religious fervor. More recently, snake handling churches in the American South have drawn attention for their seemingly outlandish worship, which often includes speaking in tongues and taking up and dancing with venomous snakes. Vodou and Santería, among many Afro-Caribbean religions, combine Christianity with African religious practices and also involve possession by the gods or saints. Most of these religions also feature music and dance as prominent component of the service, and it is hard not to watch a Vodou or a snake handling service and not see that these people are in a state of ecstasy as rapt as that of any Siberian shaman.

The most active, living sectors of Christianity in the twenty-first century are those where the worshipers have direct contact with God—accepting Jesus as their *personal* savior. This direct contact with the divine, with the priest(ess) acting as the intermediary who brings the deity down and facilitates interaction between the worshiper and the deity, rather than mediating, conveying the worshiper's needs to a distant, removed deity or standing in for the worshiper when contact is made with the deity, is also the basis of paganism and witchcraft. In some ways, modern paganism can be seen as a very extreme form of Protestantism—as indeed can be the case, given that there is a pagan coalition with the Unitarian Universalist Church, a church that just teeters on the brink of remaining Christian itself.

Gerald Gardner's first coven had been reluctant for him to publicize witchcraft and its beliefs for fear of persecution, both legal and social. The societal upheavals of the 1960s made "alternatives" of all kinds more acceptable, including alternative religions. Belief in alternate realities, including the supernatural, was a natural side effect of hallucinogenic drug experimentation—it was easy to believe in the Otherworld when you had been there and spoken with its inhabitants.

Yet while a larger percentage of society at large became open to alternate spiritualities, some of those in the mainstream—especially fundamentalist Christians—felt increasingly threatened by the changes in women's roles in American and European society in general and in religion in particular. Operating from the premise that Jehovah is the only god, devotion to any deity other than Jehovah could only be worship of Satan. Feminists who challenged patriarchal norms were already suspect; when feminist witchcraft began to come out of the broomcloset, some Fundamentalists made the simple equation that all feminists were witches.

Pagans reiterate endlessly that, since they are not Jews, Christians, or Muslims, they cannot be Satanists, because Satan is the embodiment of evil only in Judaism, Christianity, and Islam. Satanism is a real religion in two ways, however. There is the Church of Satan, which deliberately reverses the morality of Christianity as an act of rebellion against Christianity. Their religion could not exist if Christianity did not come first. This religion is a kind of radical materialism, holding that only the experience of the flesh is real and worthwhile, and that good works in the hopes of some vague happy afterlife is a fool's game; pleasure is the only purpose of life. They define pleasure in a purely subjective way, and if being good is pleasurable, they have no problem with it. While they believe that power, in general, is pleasurable, they do not believe that harming others is.

A completely different group, while also operating through the inversion of Christianity, comprises scattered individuals, often with mental problems, who use Satan as an excuse to be evil. They have little in common with Pagans of any type, even the Church of Satan, and much in common with serial killers and sociopaths. In the 1980s, these people often identified themselves as Satanists, offering human sacrifice to the Devil in hopes of gaining power in return; by the mid-1990s the same type of person was more likely to claim to be a vampire, committing murder in pursuit of eternal life.

Belief in widespread Satanism started to grow in the late 1970s and really bloomed in the 1980s and 1990s. People, especially young women, began claiming that their families were secret Satanists, practicing blood rituals in the deep woods or in basements, where young women were raped, impregnated, and their fetuses or newborns taken from them and sacrificed to Satan. Invariably their memories of these events came to them in a flash after years of repression, and the realization that they had been so abused was alleged to be the root cause of whatever life problems they were facing as adults. Virtually all of these Satanic abuse victims recovered their memories under hypnosis and/or under the care of a psychiatrist. Many families were torn apart by such accusations and in some cases, fathers themselves came to believe that they must have committed these acts and repressed their own memories of them.

Beginning in the 1980s, a wave of panics about Satanic ritual abuse of children washed over the United States and Britain. It began with the McMartin daycare case in Orange County, California, in 1983, which set the paradigm for most of the panics that followed. A parent became convinced that something untoward was going on at daycare (or in some other situation where children came together in groups supervised by nonparental adults). The police were called in and interviewed the first parent's child and then other children from the group with leading questions. In most cases, the children at first denied that anything untoward had happened to them, but under repeated questioning usually "admitted" that all the adults' worst imaginings were true. The initial questioning usually focused on straightforward acts of sexual abuse; the children usually added the increasingly bizarre details that led the adults in authority to infer that there was an organized Satanic cult behind the abuse.

The fact that many of the children's stories were physically and logistically impossible was invariably glossed over. These situations were blown into full-scale panics by sensationalistic media coverage. Not only parents but all adults in the community began to question their assumptions about the behavior of all people—what was going on that they didn't know about? Was their child cranky like any five-year-old coming down with a cold or was this the symptom of some deeper disturbance? Especially at a time when the whole concept of daycare was new, parents often felt a great deal of conflict over leaving their children with relative strangers while they spent the day at work. Was money worth the loss of "quality time" with their offspring? (It is interesting that daycare abuse panics decreased more or less in proportion as the financial necessity of having two wage-earners in the family increased in the 1990s.) How much did they really know about these people whom they trusted with their children's lives?

Many of the 1980s Satanic abuse panics were self-feeding. People who were themselves survivors of "normal" incest and abuse, as well as people who unequivocally believed in the existence of secretive Satanic churches that incorporated the sexual abuse and murder of children and sometimes claimed to be survivors of such abuse, contributed to the interviewing of the children. They provided the template for the authorities' suspicions and created self-fulfilling prophecies. The entire issue of the sexual abuse of children is beyond my scope here, but it seems significant that the 1980s was a time when sexual abuse of children and of women was an important topic in general. The feminist movement was particularly active in pushing for the exposure of sexual abuse in general. They demanded that blame fall squarely on the perpetrator—usually a white male, but always someone in a position of higher social status than the victim—for things that previously had been ignored or blamed on the victim. There was enough evidence of straightforward abuse of the vulnerable to turn anyone's stomach, but simultaneously there arose a series of outlandish accusations of abuse directed as secret Satanic cults. The inclusion of Satanism in the mix seems on some level to be a comment on the horror people felt about real abuse—this could not be the work of normal human beings you live and work with. The Devil must somehow be involved.

Even though popular belief in secretive societies of Satan worshipers had largely died out by the beginning of the twenty-first century, the defense in the murder case of Laci Peterson, a pregnant Modesto, California, woman who disappeared at Christmas, 2002, and whose body, along with that of her fetus, washed up on the shores of San Francisco Bay at Easter, 2003, suggested that the murderer was not Peterson's husband but rather a Satanic cult operating in the Modesto area. They drew attention to the unsolved murder of another pregnant woman, Evelyn Hernandez, whose body also washed up on the shores of the bay. Hernandez disappeared on May 1, 2002—the pagan holiday of Beltane—and Peterson disappeared on December 24, close enough to the winter solstice for Scott Peterson's defense team to raise the spectre of Satanism.

Ironically, the situation that bears the closest resemblance to the belief in a religious organization associated with sexual abuse is the revelation of widespread sexual abuse of children and young women by Catholic priests, a problem that began to emerge in the 1980s and may have been overshadowed by the Satanic ritual abuse panics. Although only a small number of priests have abused children, a series of investigative reports in *The Boston Globe* in 2002 revealed that the Church's response to complaints of abuse by parents and by the abused themselves were swept under the carpet and the guilty priests generally just transferred to another diocese where, more often than not, they continued their habits until another batch of complaints led to another transfer.

The revelations of sexual abuse within the Catholic Church provide some useful correctives to assertions that had been made about Satanic ritual abuse. First of all, those who had been abused by priests did not repress their memories, only to have them suddenly pop up in therapy years later. The problem facing the abused was more one of trying to forget. Those who entered therapy were very clear about their feelings of victimization and betrayal by men they were trained to regard as the earthly representatives of God. Secondly, the abusive priests were an extremely small percentage of the overall number of priests. The Catholic Church does not exist for the purpose of supplying youthful flesh for depraved sexual tastes, but rather, men with a predisposition to take advantage of a position of authority to satisfy their sexual urges gravitated toward a powerful institution that sheltered them when they were caught. (It is important to remember that, although homosexual pedophilia received the most outraged reportage, many priests sexually abused women, both children and adults.) And while the priests took advantage of their religious authority to pressure their victims into silence, it does not seem that the sexual acts themselves were given any religious over-tones.

In many ways, this priestly sexual abuse is no different from any other sexual abuse in which a person uses personal or institutional power to obtain sex from unwilling but less powerful victims. Sexual abuse of students by teachers and professors, or of workers by bosses, follows the same pattern. In situations where women have achieved positions of power, they have been known to take the same advantages as men if they can. As feminists pointed out in trying to reform social attitudes toward rape and its victims, rape is not about sex, it's about power. The added offensiveness of the Catholic scandal derived from the fact that their priests are supposed to be celibate and to provide a role model of moral rectitude for their parishioners.

In contrast, pagan religions that include sexual activity as part of their rituals may practice their rites in private, but not in secret, and their focus is on sexuality as a relationship between equals. The "power" generated by sex is for the use of the deity, not (at least in theory) to increase or demonstrate the power of one of the partners. Although the misuse of positions of status for one's own sexual ends is not unknown in the Wiccan and Pagan community—there are frequently comments about priests or priestesses whose opposite number is just by coincidence always young and beautiful—the community is also generally quite vocal that this is bad behavior, and their openness about the place of sex in the religion makes such abuses of power fairly obvious.

At the beginning of the twenty-first century, it is increasingly possible to be a witch in a liberal, most likely urban or suburban area of North America or Europe with little fear of direct harm. In less flexible or open-minded areas, while witches may not be in danger of lynching, they are in danger of having their children taken from them by governmental agencies and of other degrees of harassment if their religion becomes known. The mythology of the witch as a threat to everything wholesome and civilized is still operative. Science and technology have made life less subject to the inexplicable misfortunes that were traditionally laid at the feet of witches. Most people don't own cows any more, and if there's no milk, they're apt to blame striking teamsters and supermarket cashiers. Impotence is something to be solved with a pill, and infertility is treated in clinics. Nonetheless, the witch can still be seen as the archetypal image of vague and sinister threat.

More positively, witches and other pagans are associated with ecological concerns and generally liberal politics. The medical healing practiced by premodern folk magicians has evolved into more metaphysical healing of the planet's human-caused illnesses—pollution, global warming, and so on. A survey of 2,089 North American witches and pagans undertaken in 1993 shows that their political opinions are much more liberal than the country at large. For instance, more than 80% of those surveyed agreed or strongly agreed that there should be an Equal Rights Amendment to the US Constitution, over 84% that same-sex marriage should be legal, and 89% that there should be no discrimination on the basis of sexual preference (Berger, Leigh, and Shaffer 2003, pp. 18-20). Nearly 90% are registered to vote, just over 70% voted in the last national election, and just under 50% voted in their last local election; almost 43% are registered as Democrats and almost 28% as Independents, while only about 7% are Republicans (ibid., p. 56, 99). Compared to 55.7% of the general public, 92% of witches and pagans think that the government spends too little on the environment (ibid., p. 61).

> We find that on the whole Neo-Pagans are more liberal than the general American public but have lower confidence in government and social institutions. Neo-Pagans are also, on the whole, more politically active than the average American.... [O]ur data indicate that Goddess Worshipers, particularly women Goddess Worshipers, are among the most politically active Neo-Pagans.... [T]he three primary forms of Neo-Paganism—Wiccans, Pagans, and Goddess Worshipers—appear to be remarkably similar [demographically]. (ibid., pp. 224-226).

Given the bad reputation ascribed to the concept of the witch since the beginning of written records, it is perhaps most interesting that over 75% of those surveyed by Berger, Leach, and Schaffer, and an even larger percentage of the women, strongly believed that the label of "witch" should be retained by modern pagans (ibid., p. 228-229). Most twenty-first century witches accept that their religion per se is a relatively recent invention and does not derive from a Paleolithic or Neolithic religion retained in secret throughout two millennia of Christian persecution. They agree that the people murdered in the witch hunts were not witches in either the folk or the modern pagan sense.

Their fondness for the word "witch," then, is as symbolic as its use by contemporary Fundamentalists: yes, we are not Christians, we do not conform to patriarchal power relationships, we don't like the way modern Western society is going, and we're opting out to create the world we prefer.

CHAPTER 10

FROM SALEM TO SUNNYDALE

FROM THE VERY BEGINNING OF FILM HISTORY, the creation of "special effects" has been central. In the nineteenth century, spiritualism went hand-in-hand with the production of spirit photographs, which were inadvertently or deliberately created through flaws in processing the film. Georges Mélies's *A Trip to the Moon* (1902) was one of the most sophisticated early uses of double-exposure, stop-action, and other techniques to create a magical, fantastic world. The much-debated photographs of the Cottingly Fairies, taken in 1917 by two English schoolgirls, appeared to show the girls surrounded by delicate Otherworldly beings, although to modern eyes, inured to the use of Photoshop and other processes of image manipulation, they look quite evidently like cut-out illustrations posed around real children.

Witches per se were not prominently represented in early film, however. A number of movies used the Salem Witch trials as a background for a stereotypical lover-in-peril plot. Films were made of L. Frank Baum's Oz stories by himself and by others, and witches featured in all of these as villians, but Oz was small potatoes in the movie industry until 1939. The horror movies of the 1930s and 1940s usually featured monsters of various stripes as the source of cinematic evil. Some, such as Frankenstein and the Invisible Man, were the products of mad scientists, expressing cultural anxiety about the possible side effects of technology. Mad scientists were also fond of injecting beautiful young women with monkey hormones and other quasi-medical substances that blurred the line between nature and culture. The creatures of folklore who peopled the horror films also blurred that line—Dracula, with his ability to transform into a bat, and the Wolfman, the tragically doomed werewolf. The Mummy came closest to a being who practiced magic, and his Egyptian origin synched with the early twentieth century exaltation of ancient Egypt as the source of all magic, but his was a ritual magic, more akin to the Order of the Golden Dawn than to the folk magic of witches. Nonetheless, by mid-century witches were popular characters in film and, later, television.

The vaguely screwball-comedy witch emerged in *I Married a Witch* (1942), continuing in *Bell, Book, and Candle* (1958) and in television's *Bewitched* (1964-1972). *I Married a Witch* begins at Salem, where a lovely young witch, Jennifer (Veronica Lake), and her father Daniel (Cecil Kellaway) are burned at the stake at the instigation of Jonathan Wooley (Frederic March). They curse the Wooley men to always marry the wrong woman. In the 1940s—complete with many details of life on the home front during World War II—Jennifer and Daniel are released from the oak tree where their souls have been trapped for 270 years and decide to meddle even further in the love life of politician Wallace Wooley, Jonathan's look-alike descendent. He is about to marry Estelle Masterson, and so Jennifer tries to disrupt his marriage by making him fall in love with her by means of a love potion. Predictably, Jennifer ends up drinking the potion herself and wackiness ensues.

Bell, Book, and Candle also involves witches messing around with love spells. Gillian Holroyd (Kim Novak) is the owner of an art gallery specializing in African and other "primitive" art. She's independent, iconoclastic, goes barefoot at every opportunity, and oh yeah, she's a witch—as are her aunt Queenie (Elsa Lanchester) and brother Nicky (Jack Lemmon). Gillian lives behind her gallery, while her aunt and brother live in apartments upstairs, as does new tenant Shepherd Henderson (James Stewart), a publisher. Discovering that Shep is engaged to Merle Kittridge (Janice Rule), a woman who made Gillian's life hell at Wellesley by snitching on her (and everyone else), Gillian decides to put a spell on Shep to make him love her instead. Everything goes fine until Gillian falls in love with him herself. It appears that witches cannot love and cannot cry. When Shep is reluctantly persuaded of her magical powers and realizes that he had not fallen in love of his own free will, he leaves her. After some time has passed, however, he stops by the gallery to discover that she is now selling whimsical seashell ornaments—symbolic of her new access to the ocean of human emotion—and dressing in feminine, full-skirted dresses with Peter Pan collars and pumps, rather than capris, turtle-necks, and barefoot. She's become a human woman! She loves, she cries, she knows she done wrong! What can he do but take her back?

Both of these movies present witches who are ultimately over-powered by their own magic. They think they are in control of their emotions but they are not. They pay the price for creating unreal love but are finally rewarded with real love. In order to retain real love, they must forgo (willingly or not) the practice of magic, but in each case there are other members of the family carrying on the magical tradition as before. This ever-so-slightly undercuts the "happy" ending in which society's norms are reaffirmed in the establishment of a standard male-dominated couple. In *I Married a Witch* it is clear that one of Jennifer's daughters is carrying on in her mother and grandfather's footsteps, and Daniel himself, having been trapped in a bottle of booze when he threatened to prevent Jennifer and Wally's marriage, is an evil genie just waiting for an unlucky innocent to let him out. As for *Bell, Book, and Candle*, there is an entire subculture of witches going its merry way without Gillian, including especially her brother Nicky.

Jennifer and Daniel are not only the only witches in *I Married a Witch* but also are literally survivals from an earlier, less enlightened time. Their existence requires the belief that the witches of Salem were, indeed, practitioners of magic, capable of shape-shifting, flying with and without brooms, mixing effective potions, and cursing. They are spiteful and vindictive, delighting in causing misery for its own sake. The schism between Jennifer and Daniel occurs when Jennifer, under the power of her own magic, loses the desire to cause harm. Daniel, who has hitherto appeared to be a relatively harmless wacky drunk, is revealed to have a real streak of meanness in him; he may have no incentive to promote Wooley's happiness, but he is determined to thwart his daughter's as well. Jennifer and Daniel constantly trick each other as well as the humans; there is no honor among witches.

Bell, Book, and Candle, for its part, provides an entire witchy world that bears a remarkable resemblance to the subculture of the Beats. They wear funky, casual clothes and don't care whether they conform to social rules. They gather in basement nightclubs and listen to jazz; Nicky is a feckless bongo-player in a band. When Shep and Merle show up at the club, they are obviously slumming. Merle is an artist, but of a very classy sort (as befits a Wellesley grad): her studio is in her uptown apartment and she paints with a clean, well-pressed smock protecting her exquisite designer ensemble. There is not a speck of paint about her person, except on her perfectly made-up face. Shep, for his part, doesn't care about the factual accuracy of the books he publishes as long as they sell well. He is a publisher as a businessman, not as a midwife to the arts. The subplot of the movie concerns Sidney Redlitch (Ernie Kovacs), a writer of popular anthropological works on magic in exotic locales such as Haiti and Mexico, whom Shep very much wants as one of his own authors. Gillian performs a spell to bring Redlitch to him; this proves to be her downfall, however, as Nicky sees the chance of making a bit of money by collaborating with Redlitch on an exposé of Manhattan witch life, which leads to the necessity of Gillian revealing her identity and her activities to Shep.

Although Gillian has one foot in the mainstream world—she did, after all, go to Wellesley and she runs a successful if artsy business—her magic is very old-fashioned. She has a familiar, a cat named Pyewhacket; once she loses her magical powers, however, her cat deserts her for Queenie, who is not much of a witch, but better than nothing. One of Gillian's best bits of magic was to create a season of endless thunderstorms to torment Merle, who can't bear thunder, their senior year as retaliation for Merle's snitching: the classic witchy ability to raise storms and control the weather. Her spell to bring

Redlitch to New York involves painting a magical liquid on a picture of the author and burning it. She seduces Shep with incense and hypnotic music. The key to the success of her magic, however, is that she, personally, not particularly care about its outcome. To steal Shep from Merle out of spite is acceptable, but as soon as Shep means something to her, person to person, she has lost her power. Her relatives, less talented than she, can't understand why she would want to give up her magical power in return for love.

Nicky, willing to double-cross his sister and expose his culture to possibly dangerous outside interest as long as he benefits, is a classic self-involved magician. Although he appears fond of his sister, there is a sense that it is her magical power makes her worth his while, and it is implied that he has somewhat dropped her at the end of the movie when her powers are gone. Queenie, for her part, knows that love is supposed to be quite nice, but she just doesn't get it—as she doesn't get many things. The other witches encountered, especially Bianca de Passé (Hermione Gingold) who cures Shep of the love spell, are also concerned very much with status, which is acquired by performing magical acts that are beyond the abilities of others.

Both *I Married a Witch* and *Bell, Book, and Candle* present witchcraft as an inherited talent, if not an outright racial characteristic as explicit as black skin or epicanthal eyelid folds. At the same time, witches can pass for human, and often do. Another useful analogy is to Jewishness but not to Judaism. If you are born a witch, you are always a witch, even if you cease to practice witchcraft, even if you "convert" to humanity. However, witchcraft is never presented as a religion. The tension between witch society and human society is the central dilemma facing Jennifer and Gillian. Witches constitute an underground culture within human culture—literally, in the case of *Bell, Book, and Candle*'s Zodiac Club—with the potential to undermine it from within. While some witches are more talented than others, any learning they acquire is in how to utilize the power that is innate within them. Learning alone is not sufficient to practice magic. Mrs. De Passé, something of a social climber, does magic for mortals for a price, but the other witches in both movies seem to practice simply for their own benefit and evil amusement. They are more concerned with causing mischief than in any financial reward for their skills. The role of witches is generally to cause chaos rather than the more traditional role of stealing fertility.

The television series *Bewitched* is based on the same human-witch romantic relationship and culture clash, but with a slightly different bias. Darrin Stephens (Dick York, then Dick Sargent) marries the enchanting Samantha (Elizabeth Montgomery) only to discover that she is literally enchanting—a witch. In true paterfamilias fashion, Darrin forbids his wife to use magic in any way. In this fictional universe, witches constitute a separate society, removed from the human world, and Samantha's family is appalled that she would voluntarily succumb to human rule. The series is something of an extension of the situation of *Bell, Book, and Candle*—what was Gillian's life like after she happily-ever-aftered with Shep? Samantha does not lose her powers, however; she voluntarily commits to doing things the human way rather than taking the easy way out in terms of housework and so on. Nonetheless, each week Samantha was forced to use magic in some way, either to help her hapless husband succeed in his career as an advertising executive under the neurotic eye of his boss, Larry Tate (David White), or to remedy the wacky situations created by her mother Endora (Agnes Moorehead) and other relatives.

As a witch who chooses to be human, Samantha is the most sane, competent, and level-headed character in the series. Darrin, who would probably be a fairly normal guy if he hadn't stumbled onto the existence of witch society, is in a constant state of turmoil, outrage, or victimization as a result of his interactions with witches. Samantha's family ranges from outright malicious toward her new family— Endora is the mother-in-law from hell to end all mothers-in-law from hell—to completely incapable of comprehending how human society works, especially that magic is inappropriate. Like Aunt Queenie, they just don't get it. Although her life as a housewife, mother, and helpmeet seems cringingly oppressive in light of the subsequent feminist movement—this is precisely the "feminine mystique" that Betty Friedan tried to explode in her bestseller, published the year before *Bewitched* first aired—Samantha's ability to live in two worlds makes her stronger than any of the characters who live only in one.

The witchcraft in *Bewitched* is innate and hereditary, just as in *Bell, Book, and Candle* and *I Married a Witch*. In fact, witches don't even have to perform complicated spells in the *Bewitched* world. They wave their hands or twitch their noses and physical reality conforms with their will. Sometimes a quatrain or two is added, but the use of magical ingredients (the classic eye of newt and toe of frog, and so on) is virtually nonexistent, unless, of course, the plot requires a spell to go awry when the wrong person drinks the potion. (The latter plot device dates back at least to the numerous medieval versions of the Tristan legend, and indeed it is love potions that usually wind up in the wrong person's glass.) Samantha's nose twitch is more similar to Jeannie's crossed arms and blink in *I Dream of Jeannie* (1965-1970) and Uncle Martin's antennae in *My Favorite Martian* (1963-1966) than to traditional witch spell casting; all three are also more similar to the act of waving the fairy's magic wand than to spell casting. The idea of witches as somehow a race apart from although coexisting with humans, although looking human and capable of mating with humans, is also more of a fairy characteristic than one of witches.

Screwball witch comedies present witches as forces of chaos that upset orderly human society, fickle and malicious but ultimately incorporable into that society. The structure of the comedy genre begins with a society that is orderly yet somehow stagnant and unable to grow. Chaos erupts—or wackiness ensues—disrupting order, and then society recrystallizes in a new orderly structure that does hold the possibility of new growth, usually in the form of a fruitful marriage or two.

A Midsummer Night's Dream is a classic example of this structure. There are various couples who are prevented from marrying happily; (fairy) magic intervenes, breaking the inflexible structures creating this situation by making everyone fall in love with the wrong person; the (selective) lifting of the spells allows the couples to re-form in configurations that allow everyone to marry happily and the next generation can be produced. In *A Midsummer Night's Dream,* Titania, the fairy queen, falls victim to the love spell cast by her husband, but in witch comedies, it is usually the witch who falls victim to her own spell. Likewise, while *A Midsummer Night's Dream* ends with the reseparation of the two worlds, fairy and human, that have become chaotically mixed as a result of magic, witch comedies end with the (female) witch removed from her alien culture and incorporated into human culture, firmly under the direction of a (male) authority figure.

When the story ends with the union of the witch and the human, the overt message that human rules have tamed magical chaos is undercut by the continuing existence of other witches (Nicky and Aunt Queenie) or even more amusingly disturbing, the birth of children who have inherited this magical taint. A sitcom like *Bewitched*, however, is based on the premise that the threat of magic/chaos never goes away and must be repelled each week like clockwork. Even though the overall conflict between male human society and female witch society is more extreme in *Bewitched*, the serial nature of the narrative also keeps emphasizing the impossibility of ever overcoming magic's threat. For all of Samantha's good intentions, she keeps using magic, and for all of his demands that she not use magic, Darrin sticks around.

Witches in horror films are, not surprisingly, much more menacing, but also rather more diverse. Although the men in witch comedies put up a show of skepticism about the reality of witchcraft, they are generally convinced relatively quickly when magic is clearly demonstrated. The men in witch horror films are more wedded to their rationalism or, as becomes clear through the development of the plot, more deeply in denial. Darrin Stephens forbids his wife to practice magic but then has to put up with all the little accidents that make magic necessary, and all is resolved by the end of the episode. Professor Norman Taylor (Peter Wyngarde) in *Burn, Witch, Burn!* (1962; also known as *Night of the Eagle*) forbids his wife Tansy (Janet Blair) from practicing witchcraft, and his insistence has nearly fatal results for both of them.

Taylor is a professor of sociology, although he appears to specialize in a cross between psychology and folklore, particularly the psychology of belief in the supernatural. He is a complete rationalist: The first shot of the film shows him writing "I DO NOT BELIEVE" on the blackboard during a classroom lecture. Tansy, however, does believe. As he discovers, she had learned witchcraft from a local priest named Corrubias while they were living in Jamaica two years previously. She has been using charms and counterspells to protect the two of them from the malicious witchcraft of Flora Carr (Margaret Johnson), wife of Taylor's main competitor for chair of the department. You can tell Flora is evil because she's dowdy, somewhat cockeyed, and has a limp. In fact, she appears to be partially paralyzed on one side, a physical manifestation of the emotional paralysis associated symbolized by witches. She may even be a victim of a stroke—the inexplicable ailment caused by the malignant fairy touch.

When Norman forces Tansy to burn all her charms and amulets, his life begins to fall apart very quickly. An infatuated student first makes a sexually aggressive phone call to him and, when he rejects her, accuses him of rape. He is almost run over by a truck. The student's boyfriend, who already felt that the professor was treating him unfairly in class, first tries to blackmail him into giving him a better grade and then goes after him with a pistol to avenge his girlfriend's honor. Then a mysterious tape of Norman lecturing, with a weird interference signal in the background, arrives in the mail. Tansy knows that this is a curse that will lead to Norman's death and makes a deal with the deity who is evidently behind it all to take her life instead of his—the ritual that first introduced her to magic in Jamaica.

Norman rescues Tansy from her attempted self-sacrifice, but he still believes that everything going on is attributable to psychology and false belief. When he goes to the school and finally confronts Flora, however, she first taunts him by building a house of Tarot cards topped by a card to represent Tansy and sets it on fire, then broadcasts the mind-altering lecture tape over the public address system so that he finds himself chased and attacked by a monstrous bird, the school's mascot. He winds up in his classroom, back against the blackboard, his shoulders erasing the "not" in his statement "I DO NOT BELIEVE." At the last moment, Flora's husband shows up in her office and innocently breaks the spell. Norman makes it home to find the house in flames but Tansy safe, while Flora is crushed to death by the stone eagle over door to the school chapel. The credits roll under the caption, "DO YOU BELIEVE?"

Flora explicitly refers to magic as a religion, and women's magic is deliberately contrasted with men's science as innate modes of knowledge. Witchcraft is not an inherited trait except inasmuch as it is associated with women. However, Tansy learned her magic from a male. Following the social Darwinist theory of the nineteenth century, the European women and children are at the same level of social evolution as the primitive savages of Africa or, in this case, Jamaica.

(En route to saving Tansy from her self-sacrifice, Norman gets into a car accident; the other driver, whose insistence on filling out paperwork and seeing a doctor almost prevents Norman from making it in time, is Jamaican.) But magic is magic, whether European or Afro-Caribbean. There is no qualitative value judgement made on the fact that Tansy's magic is a kind of Vodou while Flora's appears to be home-grown, and each recognizes the charms and amulets used by the other for what they are.

The real contrast between Flora and Tansy is in their motivations. Tansy's concern is to protect her husband. Her very first magical act was to offer her life in exchange for his when he was gravely ill in Jamaica; her sacrifice was not, in the end, necessary that time, but she began learning how to do protective, defensive magic. Flora practices aggressive magic for the sole purpose of furthering her husband's career and, by extension, increasing her own status. The two women's names are interesting: Tansy is a kind of flower, *Tanacetum vulgare*, with a yellow flower and bitterly spicy leaves that repel insects, especially flies; the Devil in his manifestation as Beelzebub is Lord of the Flies., so the very name Tansy embodies the concept of repelling the Devil. Flora simply means "flowers" or "vegetation" in Latin, and although it may be a stretch to make the connection, she recalls in some ways the medieval Welsh character Blodeuwedd, the woman made of flowers who betrayed her husband and was turned into an owl—the bird that attacks Norman in the empty school.

Curse of the Demon (1957; also known as *Night of the Demon*) focuses on a male magician, the sinister Dr. Julian Karswell (Niall MacGinnis) who is the priest of the "Karswell Devil cult" located somewhere within easy driving distance of both London and Stonehenge. He has passed a slip of paper with runic symbols to an academic investigator of the occult, Henry Harrington (Maurice Denham); this written curse, which appears to have a life of its own, tosses itself in the fire and the recipient dies within a predetermined number of days at the claws of a huge, somewhat dragon-like demon. The only way to evade the curse is to pass the slip of paper back to its originator without his knowledge. Harrington was in the process of preparing a paper for an conference on Investigation of International Reports of Paranormal Phenomena, and the investigation of his death falls to his co-author, the American Dr. John Holden (Dana Andrews)—a man who shares his personal motto with the state of Missouri: "Show Me."

Curse of the Demon is based on a short story called "Casting the Runes" (1908) by M. R. James (www.fadl12200.pwp.blueyonder.co.uk/ mrjframes.html). The contrasts between the story and the movie are instructive in how popular views of magic had changed over the course of fifty years. The Karswell of "Casting the Runes" has submitted a paper on alchemy to a scholarly association and been rejected; the secretary of the society learns from acquaintances who live near Karswell that he is an unpleasant neighbor who has "invented a new religion for himself," enjoys terrorizing the local children, and has written an "evil" book on the history of witchcraft: "The man believed every word of what he was saying, and I'm very much mistaken if he hadn't tried the greater part of his receipts." A man who had given the book a scathing review died shortly afterward in a strange accident, with a look of fear on his face. The story focuses on Dunning, the man who had recommended rejecting the alchemy paper, and how he manages to turn the tables on Karswell with the assistance of the brother of the first dead man.

Karswell in the short story is a historian and alchemist who appears to have created a religion in the style of Aleister Crowley, the "wickedest man alive." Crowley began his study of magic as a rebellion against his strictly, puritanically religious family. He was initiated into the Order of the Golden Dawn and became well known in magic circles for his skill in the Order's style of ritual magic. Eventually, however, he wanted to go further and darker, particularly in the direction of sex magic, and founded several magical orders: the *Argentinum Astrum*, the Ordo Templi Orientis, and the Abbey of Thelema.

In the first part of his life, he was wealthy, successful, and talented, but with age he was overcome with drug addictions and financial setbacks that slowly turned him into a rather sad old man with a reputation for wickedness that far outstripped his capacities. His magical investigations and the structure of the organizations formulated in his prime, however, had an enormous influence on the development of Wicca through Gerald Gardner (Booth 2000). James's Karswell is a Crowley-esque figure of ritual wickedness.

The movie *Curse of the Demon* was made three years after the publication of *Witchcraft Today* and in it Karswell's religion has turned into a Wicca-esque "Old Religion." Aside from Karswell, its practitioners consists of a family straight out of Stella Gibbons's *Cold Comfort Farm* (1932), all of whom appear to have seen something nasty in the woodshed repeatedly, and over innumerable generations. It seems odd that the owner of a mansion like Lufford Abbey would be involved in any activity with such earthy types, but it turns out that he started out as a circus clown, "Dr. Bobo, the Magnificent." His wealth is all due to his worship of the demon and maintained by periodic sacrifices chosen by lot and identified by passing the runes. In the Karswell Devil cult, Nordic runes, the Christian Devil, and Neolithic Stonehenge, with its later druidic associations, are all linked together as one universal and generic paganism. However, unlike Wiccans, their horny deity is the Christian Devil, an evil spirit whose representation, as the scholars realize, has remained consistent from the beginning of recorded time and throughout the world (a kind of Bad Theosophy).

In the short story, the reviewer, Dunning, is delivered from his predicament by Harrington, who has been waiting for a chance to avenge his brother's death. The exact means of death is also left horrifyingly vague; even when Karswell succumbs to the re-passed runes, he is crushed by a falling church gargoyle (exactly as Flora dies in *Burn, Witch, Burn!*). In the movie, Holden is egged on to take the magic seriously by Joanna Harrington, niece of the dead man. Holden is a university professor; Joanna is a kindergarten teacher. Holden has a professional interest in maintaining his skepticism, while Joanna believes that children (like women and savages) are in closer touch with the reality of the supernatural and its horrors. The magic itself is not gender-specific. There is no goddess to be worshiped, only a big rubber demon mounted on squeaky wheels.

A somewhat superfluous scene in the middle of the movie takes place at a seance. Karswell's mother (Athene Seyler), worried over what her son has gotten himself involved with, asks Holden and Joanna to meet her at a house that turns out to be owned by a medium, Mr. Meek (Reginald Beckwith, who coincidentally plays one of Norman Taylor's colleagues in *Burn, Witch, Burn!*). She hopes that by contacting the spirit of Joanna's uncle they will gain insight into how they can save themselves from Karswell's runes. Mrs. Karswell's spiritualism is shown as somewhat quaint and old-fashioned, a piece with the lady herself. She is also basically good-hearted, if somewhat confused, and just wants everyone to be happy and have children (when she first meets Joanna Harrington, she first asks whether she's married and then tries to fix her up with her son). Although nothing is stated explicitly, however, there is an implication that Mrs. Karswell's "harmless" dabbling in spiritualism may have led to her son's more dangerous involvement with Devil worship.

James's original story is framed as a conflict between good scholarship and bad scholarship. Given that the events of the story show that magic itself is real, the difference between good and bad can only be seen in the ends to which the scholarship is put. Good scholarship seeks to understand the world, bad scholarship seeks to dominate it and manipulate it to its own ends. In *Curse of the Demon*, this conflict is refigured into one between science and religion. The stereotypes of the brashly empirical American, the superstitious Irishman, and the mystical Indian are put to good use. Since this is a horror movie, it is the American worldview that is proved wrong in the end, and the movie concludes that "Perhaps there are some things it is better not to know."

Although there are great benefits of wealth and power to be had from Karswell's religion, they come at the price of selling one's soul to the Devil, or at least taking out a reverse mortgage on it. The theme of selling one's soul to the Devil also forms the kernel of *Psychomania* (1971), one of the stranger movies of the psychedelic era. Here, again, there is a link between spiritualism and Satan. Mrs. Latham (Beryl Reid), a successful medium, obtained her powers by offering to the Devil the soul of her infant son Tom (Nicky Henson). The ceremony, seen in a flashback, took place at a stone circle called the Seven Witches where the now-adult Tom and his motorbike gang, the Living Dead, hang out. Tom discovers that the way to gain eternal life is to commit suicide while really, really, really believing that you will come back. Apparently there's only one death per customer. Eternal life, then, comes down to a matter of faith, as seen when one of the gang kills himself while harboring doubts and fails to rise again. The mechanisms underlying this process become somewhat clearer when it is revealed that Shadwell (George Sanders), the Latham family butler, is in fact the Devil.

A more ironic take on soul-selling and the whole Faust legend is the basis of *Bedazzled* (1967). Hapless and suicidal short-order cook Stanley Moon (Dudley Moore) sells his soul to the Devil (Peter Cook) in return for seven wishes, with which hopes to win the love of the object of his unrequited affections, Margaret (Eleanor Bron). Playing on the idea that the devil's in details, the Devil, a.k.a. George Spiggott, grants each wish exactly as Stanley enunciates it, but each time includes an additional twist that will prevent the two from having a happy life together. When Stanley hopes to wow Margaret with his intellect, she is wowed, but she is repulsed by the thought of a physical relationship. When Stanley wishes to be wealthy and for her to be affectionate, she turns out to be a gold-digger with an eye for every man except him. When he asks that they be rapturously in love *with each other*, she turns out to be married to his best friend. Finally, when Stanley thinks he has finally figured out every detail to create a perfect life for himself and Margaret, they both become trampoline-leaping nuns. Along the way, we see all the little ways in which the Devil makes life that much more annoying, creating scratches in brand-new records, disrupting phone service, expiring parking meters before their time, conning a little old lady with the promise of a promotional advertising prize. He's a petty Satan, more interested in small sins of avarice than in big, sweeping evil.

The final twist is that Satan and God are in a contest to see who can accumulate a certain number of souls to their side first. George is eagerly anticipating getting back into heaven, even though he was never all that content with just hanging around praising God all the time—lots of fun for God, as he demonstrates to Stanley, but fairly tedious for the angels. Stanley is Spiggott's winning soul, and in an uncharacteristic moment of charity, George lets him off—all his wishes are erased and he's back exactly where he started, mooning over Eleanor at the Wimpy's. The joke is on George, however, because God decrees that that one act of kindness eliminates Stanley from the total tally. George's only chance of getting back into heaven is to get Stanley to re-sell his soul, but Stanley has learned his lesson.

Movies like *Burn, Witch, Burn!* and *Curse of the Demon* are fairly vague about source of witches' evil—yes, there are demons, but are they Christian devils or primitive spirits? Representations of Original Sin, the Jungian shadow, or the Freudian id? Is evil culture-specific? *Bedazzled* shows soul-selling in an explicitly Christian context: The Devil is the fallen angel who formerly sat at the right hand of God and got kicked out of heaven for a hubristic revolt against God's authority. He wants to get back into heaven by proving himself right. He takes advantage of human emotion while remaining emotionless himself— when Stanley wishes to be an object of admiration, George makes him a rock star with hordes of swooning fans (including Margaret) who exhibit Beatlemania-esque adoration as he flings himself around the stage and screams his latest number, "Love Me!", but the fickle fans are almost immediately stolen away by George, standing very still, very cool, singing "Go away. Leave me alone. I don't love you."

But George is undone when he succumbs to emotion. He's bonded with Stanley, he's enjoyed having someone to talk to, he's in a good mood because he's going back to heaven, so why not be nice for a change? It will get him in practice for being an angel again. In the end, God is the one who comes off as petty and cold.

The pagan community at the heart of *The Wicker Man* (1973) are not witches or Wiccans, but the film has become a classic presentation of the conflict between magic and religion. Sergeant Howie (Edward Woodward) of the West Highland Police is anonymously lured to the remote island of Summerisle to investigate the disappearance of a young girl. A staunch and puritanical Christian himself, he discovers that the islanders are a unified community of practicing pagans. He has retained his virginity in anticipation of marriage; they sing lusty folksongs about the innkeeper's daughter (Britt Eklund) and fornicate in the fields to promote the growth of the crops. Their assiduity in this respect has been unsuccessful of late—the famed Summerisle harvest of apples and other produce failed the last year, and Howie comes to the conclusion that the missing girl, who had been the last harvest queen, is going to be sacrificed in hopes that the gods will grant a successful crop this year. In fact, it has all been a plot to sacrifice *him*, a man who comes of his own free will, as the representative of the King and of the law, a virgin, and a Fool.

One of the often-overlooked twists in *The Wicker Man* is that, while the islanders appear to be practicing an archaic religion that, given its uniformity throughout the community and their highly isolated location, one would assume to be an authentic survival from the pre-Christian past, Summerisle paganism is a relatively recent importation. The island had been a barren outpost in the Atlantic, surviving mostly on the fishing industry, until it had been purchased in 1868 by the grandfather of the current Lord Summerisle (Christopher Lee). That grandfather had been a hard-core scientific agronomist who wanted a place to test his new strains of plant stock. In return for their assistance in his experimentation, he allowed his tenants to return to their "old ways."

It was Summerisle's father, however, who codified the old ways into a Frazerian nature religion, complete with a provision for human sacrifice should the crops fail. Howie is sacrificed as the representative of the King, following Frazer's hypothesis of the later phase of the divine king ritual, but Howie warns Lord Summerisle that if the crops fail again after his sacrifice, the next year the islanders will have to sacrifice the real king, i.e., Lord Summerisle.

The chronology of the Summerisle family suggests that the second Lord Summerisle was indeed codifying his pagan religion at around the time that Frazer's theories were the accepted explanation of the evolution of belief (Howie even exclaims that the religion of the island is "fake biology, fake religion," paraphrasing Frazer's theory of the relationship between magic and science), that Margaret Murray was theorizing the existence of an archaic religion existing in secret especially in Scotland, and that people from the fictional Mr. Karswell to the real Mr. Gardner were creating magic-based religions of their own. Lord Summerisle is a second-generation pagan; having been raised with its tenets, he holds his beliefs as firmly as Sergeant Howie holds his.

The climax of the film is a neat reversal on the myth of the Burning Times—this time the pagans burn the Christian, pointing out to him that everyone wins here. He gets a martyr's crown, they get the blessings of Nuadu and Afallenau. They have a good point. If Sergeant Howie is as fervent a believer as he seems to be, despite the transitory pain of death by burning and smoke inhalation, he (rather than George Spiggott) will soon be spending eternity at the right hand of God. If they are as fervent believers as they claim to be, their deities will be pleased and grant them lush crops. But only if both sides are strong in their faith, whatever it may be.

The viewers of the film, however, almost always come away with a sense of horror. They see the islanders, initially, as peaceful, loving people, the counterculture stereotype of free spirits who have cast off the shackles of Establishment strictures. Sexuality, in particular, is open and celebrated. Both religions, paganism and Christianity, are ultimately revealed to be equally dogmatic but in different ways. Sergeant Howie's sacrifice is horrific only from an individualistic, humanistic point of view that views each life as sacred, its loss a tragedy, and most importantly, that does not believe in an afterlife.

The rise of interest in the supernatural and paranormal in general in the 1990s, spearheaded by the television series *The X Files* (1993-2002), coincided with an increased public awareness of Wicca and other paganisms as legitimate if non-mainstream religions. *The X Files* touched on witchcraft and Wicca on occasion, usually making a distinction between the religion and the practice of black magic or Satanism. The second-season episode "Die Hand die Verletzt" addressed Satanic ritual abuse and Satanism, with the Devil herself coming to town to exact retribution for sloppy and half-hearted worship. The Satanists are depicted as having been just another oppressed group who sought religious freedom on New England shores (a kind of reverse Puritans) and also as a completely different religion from Wicca. It runs in families only to the extent that families tend to raise their children in their own faiths, and the Devil provides benefits to the faithful such as prosperity and good health in the manner of deities worldwide. The only one to create magical effects is the Devil herself—shape-shifting, hallucinations, causing whirlpools to twist backward, falls of frogs from the sky, and the production of an enormous, man-eating python.

The television shows *Sabrina, the Teenage Witch* (1996-2002) and *Charmed* (1998-present) depict witchcraft as an inherited talent. Sabrina (Melissa Joan Hart) and the Halliwell sisters Phoebe (Alyssa Milano), Piper (Holly Marie Combs), and Prue (Shannon Doherty, later replaced by Rose MacGowan as Paige) all discover their powers at a relatively advanced age—adolescence for Sabrina, young adulthood for the Halliwells. Magic is thus presented as a metaphor for the powers and responsibilities of growing up. Both shows emphasize that magic is not something to be taken lightly and that its practice has consequences. Sabrina's witch inheritance comes through her father's side, interestingly enough, while the Halliwells are the descendants of a long line of female-only witches. Indeed, in the Halliwell's witchcraft world, the chief enemies of female witches are male warlocks, and the three Charmed Ones are destined to protect the innocent from evil.

Among the most interesting representations of witchcraft in mass media is that of Willow Rosenberg (Alyson Hannigan) on the series *Buffy the Vampire Slayer* (1996-2003), because she does not start out as a witch at all. Willow is introduced as the stereotypical girl nerd, able to tutor any student in any subject but particularly good with computers. She is also explicitly identified as Jewish, celebrating Hanukkah rather than Christmas and worried what will happen if her father finds out that she has a cross nailed next to her window to repel vampires. Of course, she also starts out heterosexual. All things change with time.

The focus of *Buffy the Vampire Slayer* is Buffy Summers (Sarah Michelle Geller), the one girl in all the world chosen to fight vampires and keep the forces of evil at bay. Slayers are chosen sequentially, a new one arising at the moment the old one dies, as all inevitably die in the line of duty. Slayers are also supposed to work in secret, their identity only known to their Watcher and to the Watcher's Council. To call Buffy an iconoclast is an understatement, however, and almost immediately upon arriving in Sunnydale, California, which is incidentally the site of a Hellmouth and thus highly attractive to vampires and all other manner of supernatural beings and occurrences, Buffy's true identity becomes known not only to her Watcher, Rupert Giles (Anthony Stewart Head) but also to her classmates Xander Harris (Nicholas Brendon) and Willow. These two become her support group, a.k.a. the Scooby Gang.

Willow's role, therefore, is to assist Buffy with the knowledge, which she initially does with inspired computer hacking (she's the only girl in school who has the city morgue bookmarked on her computer). One of the ongoing themes of *Buffy the Vampire Slayer* and its spin-off series *Angel* is the relationship between science and magic. Buffy is clearly aligned with the magical world. Her destiny is to patrol the boundaries between the human and demon worlds, and her particular focus is on vampires, beings who straddle these boundaries as human bodies infected with demon souls. At the beginning of the series, therefore, Willow the modern scientist provides a balance to Buffy the archaic mystical warrior.

Willow becomes interested in magic through the high school computer teacher Jenny Calendar (Robia La Morte), who turns out to be a technopagan and a gypsy. Jenny as technopagan combines magic and science in one package and becomes Willow's role model, but she also ultimately succumbs to the conflict between ancient and modern, science and magic. Her tribe had cursed the evil vampire Angelus with a soul, in retaliation for his murder of a girl of the tribe in the late 1890s. Now become the conscience-stricken Angel, he fights on the side of good at Buffy's side, but there was a twisted little Faustian clause in the gypsy curse—if Angel ever experienced a moment's pure happiness, his soul was once more lost.

Now, there is almost no logic to this curse whatsoever, as Jenny realizes as soon as her uncle Enyos (Vincent Schiavelli) explains it to her. Its purpose is to cause Angelus himself to feel the anguish and torment he has caused to the gypsy tribe by killing their beloved daughter, and as long as he has a soul, he's the very model of tormented broodiness. But the moment he loses his soul (by experiencing pure happiness in having sex with Buffy), he reverts to his Angelus persona and doesn't feel the teeniest bit of torment at all. Instead, he torments everyone else, especially Buffy. The "perfect happiness" clause sounds like an exquisite added torture, but in fact it backfires all around. In the second-season episode "Innocence," Enyos announces that "It is not justice we serve. It is vengeance." The gypsies use their magic in the service of an abstract vengeance no matter what the outcome and in defiance of logic and even self-preservation. The restored Angelus promptly kills Enyos and, when Jenny tries to atone for her part in the sorry mess by reconstructing and translating the lost gypsy curse, he kills her too. Science and magic may seem similar on the surface in terms of their ability to effect change in the world, but science is governed by logic and magic is governed by emotion.

After Ms. Calendar's death, Willow takes her place both as high school computer teacher (Sunnydale High has always had a rather eccentric hiring policy) and also begins investigating the world of magic by following the links on Ms. Calendar's computer—science leads her directly to magic, linked both metaphorically and electronically. As the situation with Angelus becomes more drastic, she also discovers the disk containing the translation of the Romani curse and decides to try it. Ultimately, she succeeds, although not in time to forestall the necessity of Buffy killing Angel almost as soon as he is re-ensouled. When Willow first tries the spell, she hesitantly reads the translation while her boyfriend Oz (Seth Green) stumbles through the Latin; the second time she tries to recall the soul and hold it within the orb of Thessala before transferring it to Angel, she begins even more hesitantly—she has suffered a concussion in the meantime—but suddenly becomes visibly possessed and chants strongly in Romanian (these gypsies are from Romania as well as being Rom).

There is a subtle parallelism throughout the series between Willow and the vampire Spike (James Marsters) that begins in this episode (weirdly recapitulating the relationship between vampires and witches as "exciting Others" in eighteenth century Hungary). Willow represses her emotions to an unhealthy degree; Spike is starts out as the Monster from the Id, unable to restrain himself. Neither of them has any tolerance for boredom. As Willow takes her first step toward releasing her emotion though magic, which will ultimately lead her to attempting to destroy the world, Spike takes his first step toward saving the world by proposing an alliance with Buffy to thwart Angelus. While Spike eventually seeks a soul and attempts to become more man than monster, Willow, in an alternate universe, is a vampire, and of all the people Spike threatens over the course of six seasons, Willow is the only one he seems to seriously consider siring as a vampire.

Throughout the course of the series, Willow becomes an increasingly powerful witch, but the down side of her power is that her magic is invariably affected by her emotion. Originally, Willow is shy and her emotions make her extremely anxious. She suffers from unrequited love for Xander and refuses to act on her feelings. She proclaims in "Restless," the dream episode that closes the fourth season, "I'm very seldom naughty." However, she has a long history of spells going awry, with the predictable ensuing of wackiness. This generally happens when she performs a spell under the influence of strong emotion, most notably when her lover leaves or threatens to leave her. The first time ("Something Blue"), after Oz leaves, she tries a spell to have her will be done, in hopes of willing herself to stop her heartache. Instead, her suppressed anger at her friends is revealed—Giles goes blind, Xander becomes a demon magnet, and Buffy and her arch-enemy Spike decide to marry. Two years later ("Tabula Rasa"), as her dependence upon magic as an easy fix deepens and her lover Tara (Amber Benson) threatens to leave, Willow tries an amnesia spell. This time she wants to erase specific pain in others—Tara's pain at Willow's magic use, but also Buffy's pain at being ripped from heaven by Willow's resurrection spell. Instead, her whole bag of Lethe's bramble catches fire (an appropriate metaphor for her burning emotions) and the entire Scooby gang is afflicted with total amnesia.

By the end of the sixth season, Willow's dependance on magic has become a somewhat awkward metaphor for drug addiction and after Tara is accidentally shot by Warren (Adam Busch), the villain of the season, Willow goes on the rampage and attempts to destroy the world. The connection between emotion and magic is unmistakable, but there is also a subtle progression in the sources of Willow's magic and how each makes her feel and act. Initially, she acts out of her own, personal despair and power. She tries the same resurrection spell she used on Buffy, but is rebuffed by Osiris, the god of the passage between life and death. This is all Willow can do with her own magical power.

Next she marches over to the Magic Box magic shop and absorbs the power from all the books of dark magic held there—she places her hands on the open book and the words are sucked up from the page into her, turning her eyes and hair black. With this power, she revives Buffy (who had also been shot, but not fatally) and sets out after Warren. With this power, she is capable of tracking down Warren, torturing him, and skinning him alive. So far, she has taken justice, if vigilante justice, for Tara's death. going "by the book." Now, however, she goes after Warren's weaker partners, Andrew (Tom Lenk) and Jonathan (Danny Strong). She uses up all the power derived from the books in breaking into the jail where the two are being held and in magically commandeering an eighteen-wheeler to chase them. Next, she goes to the "hard magic" dealer Rack (Jeff Kober), the guy who got her hooked on the strong stuff, and drains him of everything he has.

With this magic in her, she threatens Buffy's little sister Dawn (Michelle Trachtenberg) and mocks Buffy's own power as Slayer and her moral attitude toward battling evil. If the magic of the books makes Willow want to "throw the book" at those she blames for Tara's death, the magic she steals from Rack instills in her his own corrupt, sociopathic, power-hungry outlook. Willow turns on her friends and nearly beats Buffy in a one-on-one match, until Giles suddenly returns from England filled with the magic of a powerful coven of witches in Devon. When Willow finally saps this magic from him, from being completely incapable of feeling empathy with others, she becomes overwhelmed by her connection to the emotions of the entire human race. This means, however, that she feels the pain of the entire human race, and this, on top of her own pain over Tara, is too much for her. She decides to put everyone out of their misery and is only stopped by Xander's steadfast love for her.

Different sources of magic have different emotional effects on the person using it. Magic is presented as a kind of essence within a being that can be sapped or transferred. The body is a conduit or a container for the movement of this power. Multiple witches pooling their resources can exponentially increase their power, as Tara and Willow discover when they first perform magic together. Magical ability in general is not gender-specific in the Buffyverse (as well as not species-specific) but most of the witches per se that are encountered are female. (A significant exception is Jonathan, who perhaps not coincidentally is also Jewish.) There is an inherited aspect to some witchcraft—Tara is the daughter of a witch, as is Amy Madison (Elizabeth Ann Allen), who begins as an innocent victim of her mother's magic in the third episode of the first season but winds up a magic addict (she introduces Willow to Rack) and malevolent witch.

However, Willow has no magic blood in her veins. Her power seems to lie in an innate ability to channel energy through herself and in having the intelligence to understand the principles that shape that energy.

One aspect of the depiction of Willow as witch that aroused concern in the Wiccan and pagan communities was the terminology for Willow's powers. For some reason, she is usually called a "Wicca," which is the name of the Gardnerian religion and not of its followers, somewhat akin to calling her a "Judaism" rather than a Jew. But more to the point, there does not seem to be a particularly religious axis to her magic, despite calling upon well-known goddesses and gods such as Hecate, Aradia, and Osiris. She even continues to refer to herself as Jewish on occasion after she is well into the practice of witchcraft.

However, religion per se is a somewhat ambiguous quality throughout the Buffyverse; crosses and holy water, for instance, have effect on vampires absolutely, regardless of the fact that most of the vampires encountered are not Catholic and vampirism is described as existing long before the advent of Christianity. Sunnydale is a town with an unusual number of churches for its size, yet they are invariably empty or destroyed. Despite the use of a religious term for Willow's witchcraft, what she practices is practical rather than spiritual.

Willow is a sympathetic character who nearly destroys the world in her grief. Her magic is "good" when she uses it to benefit Buffy and the Scoobies in the fight against evil, but "bad" when she uses it for selfish, self-medicating purposes. After her almost-apocalypse, she is so frightened of her power that she is reluctant to use it, but ultimately it is Willow, the lesbian witch, who reverses the dictates of the original male Council that only one girl in every generation becomes a Slayer, and makes it possible for every girl who could have the power to have it in fact. (During which spell her hair turns white, just as it turned black when she went evil at the end of the previous season.) But at the same time, the Slayer's role is to patrol the boundaries between the human and demon worlds, between night and day, rationality and irrationality, superego and id, and especially to kill the vampires who straddle that boundary.

Somehow, in the final battle between the Slayer(s) and the First Evil that destroys Sunnydale, the only two core characters to die are

Spike, the vampire who got a soul for Buffy's sake, and Anya (Emma Caulfield), the ex-vengeance demon whose humanity is a result of her love for Xander. They are also the two characters who most muddy the clear line between human and demon.

Willow embodies the ambivalence of magic and of witchcraft. The act of magic itself is neither good nor evil, except for the intention of the person performing the act. The magic of the Buffyverse is a natural power, in some ways no different from electricity or wind, that occurs without human intervention but which humans can learn to control. In this way, Willow the scientist and Willow the witch are exactly the same person, and if Willow the crazed, grief-stricken witch could destroy the world, so could Willow the mad scientist, if she had gone that way instead.

Nearly every witch in literature—whether oral or written, popular or elite—ends up categorized as good or evil, with no ambiguity allowed. Willow returns the witch figure to the ambiguity that characterizes Medea, the Ur-witch of Western culture. Medea originally was sympathetic as a woman who gave up everything to follow her emotions and horrific when her emotions were thwarted and she took bloody revenge, a witch whose power was valued when it benefitted the goals of men and scorned when they no longer needed it.

In a post-nuclear, post-feminist age, the dichotomies of male-female, culture-nature, science-magic, logical-emotional are increasingly hard to maintain. Willow is finally a character who is herself first, and a witch second.

CHAPTER 11

CONCLUSION

There has never been a time when people did not believe in magic. There also has never been a time when people were not skeptical about the reality of magic. What has changed over time has been the ways in which people conceptualize magic, the specifics of magical activities, who they believe practices it, and the value they place on those people. Magic is similar to fiction in that it requires imagining and inhabiting an alternate reality, and both magic and fiction (or myth) appear in the second earliest phase of writing, as soon as writing is used for anything more than simple accounting.

There is a difference between believing in magic and witches and telling stories about magic and witches, however. Beliefs about what witches do stayed very consistent, and usually involved threats to life and fertility, i.e., the production of new life. Witches are the explanation for things that can't otherwise be explained—famine, crop failure, damaging storms, infertility of humans and livestock, cows that won't give milk, butter that won't churn, bread that won't rise. All of these activities threaten the continuation of civilization, and so in a more general sense, witches are the inverse of everything beneficial in society. They represent the forces of chaos that threaten life as we know it.

Prior to the late Middle Ages, witches were universally believed to be evil beings, but they were not the only beings capable of magic. Fairies were also magical creatures who could be threatening—especially when it came to stealing healthy babies and leaving sickly changelings in their place—or helpful—offering knowledge, household assistance, and riches to the humans who are nice and helpful to them. There were also humans who had knowledge of magic (sometimes acquired from fairies) that showed them where hidden treasure and stolen goods were secreted, how to heal illnesses with plants and other natural materials, how to read portents in stars and natural disasters, and other useful talents. These skills predated the establishment of Christianity and continued to be used after Europe had by and large converted. Sometimes the pagan element in this folk magic was retained in Christian times, sometimes it was completely Christianized (substituting the names of saints and angels for those of pagan deities, for instance), sometimes both Christian and pagan deities were called upon, just to be sure.

There's no simple reason why the Church became convinced that people were gaining unnatural powers by worshiping the Devil, but once the idea of diabolical witchcraft took root in the elite culture, the evil witches of the imagination and the folk healers and magicians of peasant culture were lumped together as equally threatening to Christian society. The witch persecutions of the late medieval and early modern eras united the extremes of imaginary witches with real-world effect—paranoia about diabolical witchcraft led to the torture and execution of thousands of innocent people, especially women.

The witch hunts marked a major and lasting turning point in popular beliefs about witches. Paranoia about evil witches and the equation of witchcraft with any non-Christian religion has persisted up to the twenty-first century. The Satanic ritual abuse panics are one case in point; another is the popularity of J. K. Rowling's Harry Potter books and the Fundamentalist reaction to that popularity.

Rowling's projected seven-volume series, five of which have been published as of 2003, is a coming-of-age story about Harry Potter, who is eleven years old at the beginning of *Harry Potter and the Sorcerer's*

Stone (1997). Just as he reaches the age when British children begin their secondary schooling, he discovers that his dead parents were witches and that he is about to enter Hogwarts School of Witchcraft and Wizardry. His "normal" schooling in magic consists of classes in Defense Against the Dark Arts, Herbology, Potions, Charms, Transfiguration, and the History of Magic. Magic is performed with a combination of verbal spells, the mixture of magical ingredients, and the wave of a magic wand. Magical skill is a congenital talent, but some families are full of witches—like Harry's friends the Weasleys—and some witches are born into otherwise nonmagical families, also known as Muggles. Hogwarts, however, is able to identify everyone who has magical skill, no matter what their family background, and offers them the chance to be trained.

However, in addition to his regular school work, Harry must contend with the enmity of Voldemort, the evil wizard with ambitions of world domination who killed Harry's parents and who tried to kill Harry. Why Harry did not die is one of the enduring mysteries of the magical world, but in the process, some of Voldemort's power was transferred to Harry and now Harry is the wizard with the best chance of thwarting him. Through the course of the series, Harry learns about his parents and the world they inhabited, gains increasing control over his powers, and deals with deceit, betrayal, and death.

Much of the charm of the novels lies in Rowling's imaginative creation of a magical world that coexists, unseen, with the Muggle world. Photographs and paintings in the magical world are animated, with the subjects frequently wandering out of the frame to take care of business elsewhere. Magical sweets include Bertie Botts Every Flavor Beans, a kind of extreme jelly bean that literally come in every flavor, including Brussels sprouts and ear wax. The train to Hogwarts leaves from Platform 9-3/4, and it requires walking through a brick wall to get there. Because witches can perform many things, such as communicating over long distances or traveling to far-off places, by magic, they have no need for and do not understand such Muggle technology as telephones and automobiles. Mr. Weasley, father of Harry's best friend Ron, works in the Misuse of Muggle Artifacts office of the Ministry of Magic and has an anthropological fascination with Muggle society.

The magical world is inhabited by more than witches and wizards—there are also giants, house-elves, boggarts, dragons, unicorns, ghosts, centaurs, creatures of folklore and mythology, as well as beings peculiar to Rowling's imagination, such as Dementors. Witches ride brooms in this magical universe, but mostly in order to play Quidditch, a kind of three-dimensional soccer/lacrosse hybrid. Magic is governed by a civil bureaucracy—the Ministry of Magic—and there are rules and regulations to be followed. The magical world has its own currency, its own banking system (run by goblins), its own penal system (including the dreaded prison of Azkaban), and of course its own educational system.

Part of the fun of the Harry Potter books is the way in which Rowling uses the magical world as a satire on the real world, with the same schoolchild misadventures and grown-up politics exaggerated through witchcraft. (My father described the books as *"Tom Brown's Schooldays* with magic." It remains to be seen whether some twenty-second century writer will create a series of antihero novels featuring Draco Malfoy, as George Macdonald Fraser did with Thomas Hughes's Flashman.)

The magical world of Hogwarts also has many of the more unpleasant elements of the Muggle world. While most witches are beneficent, there are those, such as Voldemort and his followers, who use magic for personal power. A faction among the wizards advocates a kind of magical racism, calling witches and wizards of mixed magical and Muggle blood "mudbloods" and wishing to banish them from the magical world. There are vain wizards who lie about their achievements, such as Professor Gilderoy Lockhart, who teaches Defense Against the Dark Arts, in *Harry Potter and the Chamber of Secrets* (1999), and silly witches who exaggerate their powers, such as Professor Sibyll Trelawney, who teaches Divination, in *Harry Potter and the Prisoner of Azbakan* (1999). In *Harry Potter and the Goblet of Fire* (2000), the children encounter racism against those of mixed witch and giant blood. In *Harry Potter and the Order of the Phoenix* (2003) there is a hospital—St. Mungo's Hospital for Magical Maladies and Injuries—for people who have been injured mentally or physically by magic gone awry.

While Harry encounters wise and helpful authority figures, particularly Professor Albus Dumbedore, the head of Hogwarts, and Professor Minerva McGonagall, head of Harry's house at school, there are also hostile authority figures, such as the school caretaker Angus Filch and his cat Mrs. Norris. Even more confusing is Professor Severus Snape, the Potions teacher, who is quite obviously hostile toward Harry personally, but whose political allegiances are nonetheless on Harry's side. One of Harry's most devastating revelations is that his idealized father had, in fact, bullied Snape ruthlessly when the two were at school. Magic, in Harry Potter's world, is as good or as evil as its caster's intent.

The Harry Potter series has been credited with inspiring a huge increase in middle-grade reading and the anticipation for publication of each new volume makes news worldwide. Rowling, who was a single mother on welfare when she wrote the first volume in the series, has become one of the wealthiest people in Britain from her writing. The extraordinary popularity of a series of novels that makes witchcraft and magic seem glamorous, exciting, and real has aroused a great deal of anxiety among Christian groups. Despite—or perhaps because of—the moral ambiguities of magic that Rowling introduces in her books, these groups see any use of magic, whether for good or evil, as a ploy to entice the unwary innocent to the practice of black magic.

Self-proclaimed occult experts, such as Caryl Matrisciana, producer of the documentary *Harry Potter Witchcraft Repackaged, Making Evil Look Innocent* (2000), claim that "Through Harry Potter books and audios, children as young as kindergarten age are being introduced to human sacrifice, the sucking of blood from dead animals and possession by spirit beings" (http://www.khouse.org/articles/personal/20011001-374.html). The moral value placed on these episodes in the narrative are irrelevant to critics; the mere fact that they are mentioned at all is believed to lure children to investigate witchcraft and become involved in the occult.

The online satirical magazine *The Onion* spoofed the anti-Harry movement with an article titled "Harry Potter Books Spark Rise in Satanism Among Children" accompanied by a picture of three kindergarten-aged children dressed in robes and pointy hats chanting around a blood-red pentagram drawn on the floor, with copies of the

Harry Potter books propped on their laps. A Christian web site counters the satire with a "That's Not Funny":

> For those of you who insist that the series is innocent fun, and even good for the children because it spurs them to read and expand their imagination, I would ask you to consider the following. First, since when has an international fad been wholesome? Usually anything truly of redeeming virtue is spurned by the world. Shouldn't that alone urge caution? Second, there are so many other books that also expand the imagination and promote reading, it is a pity to spend that energy on something that portrays witchcraft, sorcery, magic, and other occult practices as good (http://www.greaterthings.com/Lexicon/H/HarryPotter/).

The reaction to the magic in Harry Potter is not anything new,. Conservative Christian commentators have even seen J. R. R. Tolkien's *The Lord of the Rings* (1954-1955) as dangerously pagan despite the author's fervent Catholicism (http://www.crossroad.to/articles2/rings.htm). Such reactions have less to do with worry over the explicit content of stories and more with overanxious fears of where an inquiring mind, sparked by tales of magic, might be led.

Wiccan organizations such as Britain's Pagan Federation do report a significant increase in inquiries about magical training directly traceable to the publication of Harry Potter books (as well as to *Buffy the Vampire Slayer, Sabrina, the Teenage Witch*, and other popular culture depictions of witchcraft); this is one of the reasons that most Wiccan and Pagan organizations refuse to accept minors for training. Pagans themselves are torn over the popularity of Harry Potter and other such works. On one hand, they are pleased to see witches depicted as positive characters; on the other, they are also disturbed that the witchcraft of fiction has so little relationship to the Wicca and witchcraft of real life (http://www.witchvox.com/wren/wn_detail.html?id=7322). The chief difference between the magic of Harry Potter and the magic of Wicca is precisely the lack of a religious element in the novels. Witchcraft is presented as a way of life that is as inescapable as one's eye color.

How did we get from "witch" to "Wicca"? In part, science not only has replaced witchcraft as the explanation for how the world works, it also has replaced witchcraft as the explanation for misfortune. Epidemics are no longer blamed on malevolent sorcerers but on mutated viruses that have escaped from government labs. Studies prove that infertility is caused by smoking cigarettes, wearing tight underwear, excessive bicycle riding, or postponing childbearing in order to pursue a career, and science provides clinical treatments to overcome it as well. Violent storms are blamed on global warming, which in turn is blamed on the excesses of scientific technology. With the role of Source of All Evil supplanted by science, magic did a 180-degree flip and became humankind's connection to a warm and nurturing Mother Earth.

By the nineteenth century, masculine domination of both science and religion left an opening for witchcraft to fill the void in the arena of the female divine, female knowledge, and female authority. Increasing sophistication in historical research and a shift in interest from the doings of the elite to the lives of the working and peasant classes rehabilitated the importance of female healers and the folk magic they practiced and transmitted.

It is also hard to avoid the suspicion that Wicca and other modern paganisms arose precisely because mainstream Christianity had insisted for so long that they existed. From the *Canon episcopi* grilling confessants whether they rode in the night with Diana or Herodias, to Kramer and Spengler outlining the process of selling one's soul to the Devil, to Margaret Murray insisting that the witch hunts had targeted an authentic religion dating to the Paleolithic, the idea of a paganism lurking in the underbrush of European culture was part of its supporting mythology. Whether you supported or rejected Christianity, its opposite could only be witchcraft.

From the very beginning, "witch" has been a synonym for "the Other." Witches are women when the cultural norm is male; they are pagan when the cultural norm is Christian; they are spiritual when the cultural norm is materialist; they become a religion as the cultural norm turns secular; they are healers when anxiety about the medical establishment is an issue; they are environmentalists when big business has bought the government; they are magic in a world of science.

CHAPTER 12

BIBLIOGRAPHY

Aitchison, Nick. *Macbeth: Man and Myth.* Stroud, Gloucester, UK: Sutton, 1999.

Ankarloo, Bengt, and Stuart Clark, eds. *Witchcraft and Magic in Europe.* 6 vols. Philadelphia: University of Pennsylvania Press, 1991-2002.

Apollonius of Rhodes. *The Voyage of Argo.* Translated by E. V. Rieu. 2d ed. New York: Penguin, 1971.

Apuleius, Lucius. *The Golden Ass.* Translated by Robert Graves. New York: Farrar, Straus, and Giroux, 1951.

Bartel, Pauline. *Spellcasters: Witches and Witchcraft in History, Folklore, and Popular Culture.* Dallas: Taylor, 2000.

Baum, L. Frank. *Dorothy and the Wizard in Oz.* Chicago: Reilly & Lee, 1908.

_____. *Glinda of Oz*. Chicago: Reilly & Lee, 1920.

_____. *The Land of Oz*. Chicago: Reilly & Lee, 1904.

_____. *The Magic of Oz*. Chicago: Reilly & Lee, 1919.

_____. *The Wizard of Oz*. Chicago: G. M. Hill, 1900.

Bede, the Venerable. *A History of the English Church and People*. Translated by Leo Sherley-Price. New York: Penguin, 1968.

Berger, Helen A., Evan A. Leach, and Leigh S. Schaffer. *Voices from the Pagan Census: A National Survey of Witches and Neo-Pagans in the United States*. Columbia, S.C.: University of South Carolina Press, 2003.

Booth, Martin. *A Magickal Life: A Biography of Aleister Crowley*. London: Hodder and Stoughton, 2000.

Bromwich, Rachel, ed and trans. *Trioedd Ynys Prydein*. 2d ed. Cardiff: University of Wales Press, 1978.

Fletcher, Richard. *The Barbarian Conversion from Paganism to Christianity*. New York: Henry Holt, 1997.

Flint, Valerie I. J. *The Rise of Magic in Early Medieval Europe*. Princeton, N.J.: Princeton University Press, 1991.

Ford, Patrick K. *The Mabinogi and Other Medieval Welsh Tales*. Berkeley: University of California Press, 1977.

Frazer, Sir James George. *The Golden Bough: A Study in Magic and Religion*. 12 vols. London: Macmillan, 1890-1905.

Geoffrey of Monmouth. *Historia Regum Britanniae: Histories of the Kings of Britain*. Translated by Sebastian Evans, revised by Charles W. Dunn. New York: Dutton, 1958.

————. *The Life of Merlin: Vita Merlini*. Translated by Basil Clarke. Cardiff: University of Wales Press, 1973.

Graves, Robert. *The White Goddess: An Historic Grammar of Poetic Myth*. London: Faber & Faber, 1948; Rev. ed. 1966.

Hansen, George P. *The Trickster and the Paranormal*. n.p.: XLibris Corp., 2001.

Harpur, Patrick. *Daimonic Reality: A Field Guide to the Otherworld*. New York: Viking Arkana, 1994.

Henken, Elissa R. *National Redeemer: Owain Glyndër in Welsh Tradition*. Ithaca, N.Y.: Cornell University Press, 1996.

Hutton, Ronald. *The Triumph of the Moon: A History of Modern Pagan Witchcraft*. New York: Oxford University Press, 1999.

Investigative Staff of *The Boston Globe*. *Betrayal: The Crisis in the Catholic Church*. Boston: *The Boston Globe*, 2002.

Jarman, A. O. H. "Early Stages in the Development of the Myrddin Legend." In Rachel Bromwich and Brynley Roberts, eds., *Astudiaethau ar yr Hengerdd: Studies in Old Welsh Poetry*. Cardiff: University of Wales Press, 1978.

Jones, Thomas, and Gwynn Jones, trans. 1948. *The Mabinogion*. New York: Dutton, 1948.

Klaniczay, Gábor. *The Uses of Supernatural Power: The Transformation of Popular Religion in Medieval and Early Modern Europe*. Edited by Karen Margolis and translated by Susan Singerman. Cambridge: Polity Press, 1990.

Lewis, Matthew. *The Monk*. Edited by Lewis F. Peck, introduction by John Berryman. New York: Grove Press, 1952. Work originally published 1796.

Lüthi, Max. *The European Folktale: Form and Nature*. Translated by John D. Niles. Bloomington: Indiana University Press, 1982. Work originally published 1947.

Mac Cana, Proinsias. *Celtic Mythology*. Rev. ed. New York: Peter Bedrick, 1983.

_____. *The Learned Tales of Medieval Ireland*. Dublin: Dublin Institute of Advanced Studies, 1980.

McNeil, John T., and Helena M. Gamer, eds. and trans. *Medieval Handbooks of Penance: A Translation of the Principal Libri Poenitentiales*. New York: Columbia University Press, 1938.

Merrifield, Ralph. *The Archaeology of Ritual and Magic*. New York: New Amsterdam Books, 1987.

Migne, Jacques-Paul, ed. and trans. *Patrologia Latina*. Paris: Garnier Bros., 1878-1890.

Murray, Margaret. *The Divine King in England*. London: Faber & Faber, 1954.

_____. *The God of the Witches*. London: Sampson Low, Marston, 1931.

_____. *The Witch Cult in Western Europe*. Oxford: Clarendon Press, 1921.

Norton, Mary Beth. *In the Devil's Snare: The Salem Witchcraft Crisis of 1692*. New York: Alfred A. Knopf, 2002.

Oppenheim, Janet. *The Other World: Spiritualism and Psychic Research in England, 1850-1914*. Cambridge: Cambridge University Press, 1985.

Pócs, Éva. *Between the Living and the Dead: A Perspective on Witches and Seers in the Early Modern Age*. Translated by Szilvia Rédey and Michael Webb. Budapest: Central European University Press, 1999.

————. *Fairies and Witches at the Boundary of Southeastern and Central Europe*. Folklore Fellows Communication no. 243. Helsinki: Academia Scientiarum Fennica, 1989.

Pullman, Philip. *His Dark Materials* (comprising *The Golden Compass*, *The Subtle Knife*, and *The Amber Spyglass*). New York: Ballentine, 1995-2000.

Rowling, J. K. *Harry Potter and the Chamber of Secrets*. New York: Scholastic Books, 1999.

————. *Harry Potter and the Goblet of Fire*. New York: Scholastic Books, 2000.

————. *Harry Potter and the Order of the Phoenix*. New York: Scholastic Books, 2003.

————. *Harry Potter and the Prisoner of Azkaban*. New York: Scholastic Books, 1999.

————. *Harry Potter and the Sorcerer's Stone*. New York: Scholastic Books, 1997.

Thomas, Keith. *Religion and the Decline of Magic*. New York: Charles Scribner's Sons, 1971.

Tolstoy, Nikolai. *The Quest for Merlin*. Boston: Little, Brown, 1985.

Vale, V., and John Sulak, eds. *Modern Pagans: An Investigation of Contemporary Pagan Practices*. San Francisco: RESearch, 2001.

Washington, Peter. *Madame Blavatsky's Baboon: A History of the Mystics, Mediums, and Misfits Who Brought Spiritualism to America*. New York: Schocken Books, 1993.

Wood, Juliette. "Margaret Murray and the Rise of Wicca." *The Pomegranate: A New Journal of Neopagan Thought* 15 (February 2001): 45-52.

INDEX

INDEX